Me 'n Elvis

By Charlie Hodge with Charles Goodman

CASTLE **W** BOOKS

Memphis

Me 'n Elvis

By Charlie Hodge with Charles Goodman

Library of Congress Catalogue Number 84-70644

ISBN 0-916693-00-7

Premier Limited Edition

Number

ELVIS IN PARIS

Elvis jumped out of his long black limousine the moment it stopped. He went up the station steps three at a time.

The sun, slowly turning orange, eased down behind the gray stones of the old German village towers to the west of us.

The train to Paris had just pulled out.

Elvis looked down the empty platform and the vanishing railroad tracks.

"Charter us a plane," he said.

Elvis—always impatient.

The Story . . .

Me 'n Elvis

The intimate memoirs of Charlie Hodge who shared Elvis' home and his stage life for seventeen years.

"Elvis liked to introduce everyone who worked with him on stage. I always stood right next to him but I was always the very last one Elvis introduced. He would turn to me and say, 'Charlie plays acoustic guitar, sings harmony with me, gets me a glass of water and hands me the scarfs--and he is my friend.'"

—Charlie Hodge

For Punkin

Charlie Hodge

The Prelude

Lisa Marie wandered into the den.

She had that "moody Elvis" look.

There was so much of her father in her that it hurt to watch her. The same blue eyes with the low fire burning. The cat moves seen on a thousand screens and stages.

She sank down on the couch by me.

On the green lawn outside, her Grandfather, Colonel Beaulieu watched our steaks smoke and hiss on a stone firepit he brought back from a trip out to the Orient.

Mrs. Beaulieu was out in the kitchen, fixing salad and things. Looking at her profile, you could see where Priscilla got her beauty.

Dinner was to be at seven. That was the usual hour at the Beaulieu home.

"Charlie," Lisa Marie said, softly.

"Yes, 'Punkin,'" I said, taking off my reading glasses.

She dragged her toes through the thick carpet.

Elvis liked to roam the house to find someone to talk to. Often, absentmindedly, he would pick up my electric razor and knock the beard off his face while he talked.

"I was reading one of those books," Lisa Marie said. "You know. The ones that talk about Daddy."

I nodded and waited. She needed time to say it her own way.

"Those books" were the sort written quickly and shoved into print by strangers to make a fast buck after her father died.

She looked up at me at last.

I was glad to see the Presley fire flicker anew at the bottom of her warm eyes.

"Daddy could act crazy," she said. "But he didn't act the way some people say he did all the time."

1

She looked at me in silence. Vulnerable. Waiting for me to reassure her in some way.

I had stayed in Elvis' home for 17 years.

There were so many good things to tell her about her father —so many good memories.

Elvis always expected good things.

"I knew something good was going to happen to me," he said. "I just didn't know what it was. But it was a feeling that the future looked kind of bright, a feeling that I had ever since I was a kid."

Sometimes he worked so hard to make his dream come true that somebody would ask him if he wasn't taking on too big a load.

Elvis would smile and say, "This mountain is not too steep for a fine stepping horse. Don't you worry any about the hoss. Just help load the wagon."

We were both only 21 when Elvis walked out of the shadows and into my life—backstage at a big Memphis auditorium. I was singing with the Foggy River Boys on a national tour with Red Foley's Ozark Jubilee.

Uncle Sam recruited me and Elvis for basic training at the same time. He put us in neighboring barracks at Fort Hood, Texas.

Riding the high seas, aboard the troopship SS *General Randall*, Elvis had the officers put me in the bunk right above his.

At night I could hear him weeping for his mother. She lay in her fresh grave. I tried to comfort him then.

Elvis' military base in Germany was only a few miles from mine. He told me to think of the big old house he rented at Bad Nauheim as my own.

We played together in Paris on leaves.

When Elvis came back home he asked me to climb on the train with him and go to Hollywood.

When Elvis returned to the concert stage in Las Vegas, he wanted me up there with him. To help with the rough spots. To keep a glass of his Mountain Valley water from

Arkansas handy on top of the stage piano. To hand him all the scarfs he sailed out to the audience. To harmonize.

Elvis discovered that when he wanted to complain about something on stage—he could yell at me about it. That got his complaint across to everybody but it didn't make anybody mad at him, including me. I always understood what he was up to.

I grew up entertaining people by mimicking voices. I trained my voice to sound like Elvis'. When his voice got tired he could just fade away and I would pick up the note and carry it to the end. The audience never knew they were hearing my voice instead of his.

Wherever Elvis lived—in Palm Springs, Los Angeles or at Graceland—he had one room that he called "Charlie's Room."

We chased an incredible dream for 17 years. No book can capture it all. No movie.

A mystery is not easily trapped.

And Elvis was a mystery—his life baffled even him.

Coming in off a short tour, once, Elvis said, "Charlie you know how much money we made for working all of 12 hours on stage?"

We headed out the back door of Graceland toward the barn to check the horses.

"How much?" I said.

"For 12 hours of music, after paying off all our expenses, we brought home a little over $800,000!" he said.

I went upstairs to his bedroom one night at Graceland. The room was as cold as a snowfield in the Rockies. Elvis loved the air that way. One of the guys used to tell people, "It's so cold that you could hang meat in there."

I sat down on the couch by Elvis' bed and tried to keep from shivering. I had to go in his huge closet and pull down one of his robes. I wrapped it around me. It was one of those soft blue ones Elvis liked. With the hood you can pull over your head—and that's just what I did with it.

I sat back down on the end of the couch, crossed my legs like a mediating Eskimo, and smiled.

He watched me.

"Charlie," he said.

"Yea, Elvis?"

He punched the big pillow and leaned back on it.

"Did you ever stop to think what one little boy from Tupelo, Mississippi and another little boy from Decatur, Alabama have done?" he asked.

"What's that, Elvis?"

"We entertained the whole world," he said.

I nodded. "Yea." We had done more than 2,000 shows together.

Elvis looked up at the ceiling.

He stayed that way a long time.

His smile turned, slowly as twilight falling, into a faint look of puzzlement. There was a wrinkle of concentration between his eyes. I noticed a touch of gray at his temples.

I had seen that look many times before.

He shook his head. "It never ceases to amaze me."

Ready to Skyrocket

Elvis was a red hot kid, ready to skyrocket when I first met him on a shadowy backstage in Memphis. He had come downtown to see Red Foley's touring Ozark Jubilee. My Foggy River Boys were appearing on it.

Elvis came backstage to meet everybody.

One of the girls on Foley's show, Wanda Jackson, told us she had sung on the same bill with Elvis once. He was so explosive on stage that nobody wanted to follow his act.

I looked up and there was Elvis Presley. He was walking toward me near a side door where I was having a cigarette. There was a kid with him. Short, like me. A nice teenager with those friendly big eyes and a great smile that lit up the shadows. The kid tried to comb his hair the same way Elvis did—fluffed up in a high bouffant. This was Billy Smith, an Elvis cousin.

"Me and Elvis were watching, the night you guys won Arthur Godfrey's professional talent show," Billy said after we shook hands. "It was fantastic."

"You know what?" I said. "That show had me scared out of my drawers. I didn't want the Foggys to go on it at all. We were already stars. (On Foley's weekly network show on ABC television out of Springfield, Missouri.) The only thing the Godfrey show could do to us would be hurt us if we lost. And we had to go up against some big professional talent. I was dead against doing the show. All the way."

"But you guys won," said Billy.

"Thank God," I said.

I flipped my cigarette out the side door and we stood around backstage talking. I liked them both.

Elvis said he had always wanted to sing with a gospel quartet like mine. He managed to get Cecil Blackwood to listen to him sing.

Elvis smiled. "Mr. Blackwood told me I had better stick to driving my truck."

I asked Elvis if he ever caught our weekly network show.

"Just every Saturday night," he said.

Uncle Sam pulled both our names out of his tall hat at the same time in 1958.

Elvis arrived at Fort Hood for basic just about the same time I got there. He was in a barracks just down the street from mine. As soon as he moved in, I went over to say hello.

His eyes swept right over me. I was standing there in rumpled green fatigues. He showed no recognition of me at all. Nothing.

I really wasn't too recognizable. The camp barber had already given both of us crew cuts. Now, a crew cut does a lot to change your whole appearance. It may well be the best disguise ever created by man. Pictures of me that were taken then, even my mother can't recognize.

"You look real familiar," Elvis said. "I just can't place you."

"I sang lead with the Foggy River Boys," I said.

He got a big smile. "Hey man! I met you backstage at the Auditorium in Memphis." He shook his head. "I just didn't recognize you like this."

We saw each other from time to time. One weekend I saw him standing by a big red Lincoln with a Waco friend named Eddie Fadal and a couple of Elvis' employees from up in Memphis. They all piled in the big limousine and Elvis

Looking sharp with Eddie Fadal in 1956

Changing clothes
in Texas

...looking olive
"drab" with me in
1958...

drove off to spend the weekend at Fadal's big house in Waco.

I watched them drive through the main gate and on out of sight.

I got in line for the next bus and rode it into town and messed around awhile.

It was a gloomy September for Elvis.

His mother was ill. The Army gave him some time to go home to see her. She died suddenly while he was there.

Eddie Fadal told me just how grim that September was in Memphis:

Elvis was numbed by grief. We tried to take his mind off it but nothing worked.

Someone got the idea of asking the Tennessee Highway Patrol to fly in one of its helicopters.

The next day, one of the state's big choppers landed out behind the Graceland mansion. The pilot began giving Elvis and the rest rides.

They came back the next day. They kept flying Elvis all over Memphis and along the river. Tennesse loved Elvis. They grieved along with him.

The helicopter pilot avoided the Forest Hill Cemetery and that new grave.

Days passed. Still the gloom lay over Graceland like a thick mist.

One day, the helicopter pilot gave Elvis the control stick right after they took off.

"You fly it," the pilot said.

Elvis didn't hesitate a moment. He flew the chopper.

When he brought it back in to land in the field behind the

The First Class Look

mansion, Elvis looked down at all of us staring up at him solemnly.

And he smiled.

Still grieving over his mother, Elvis had to leave all his friends and relatives behind when he got on the troop train and rolled north to the port of embarkation.

That was when me and Elvis started to get close.

He was sitting staring out a train window when I went up the aisle looking for him. I sat down across from him.

We talked about this and that. About the show people we knew. It got late. I fell asleep as the train rattled and rolled along. He put a blanket over me.

Elvis came through the ship looking for me after we sailed out of the harbor aboard the troopship SS *General Randall*.

"Charlie," he said, "I don't know a single one of those guys up in my compartment. You want to move up there with me?"

He got permission from the ship's officers. I moved to his compartment. I took the bunk on top. Elvis had the bunk below.

During the days on the high seas, he was smiling and relaxed. Really easy going.

At night he grieved in his bunk. I would lie there in the darkness and listen as he quietly moaned from down in his heart. After a while, I would climb down and sit on the side of his bunk.

I'd tell him jokes and stories until he began to feel a little better and could fall asleep.

When I climbed back up in my bunk, I made it my goal to keep Elvis laughing all the way across the ocean.

One day, as we stood at the railing and the ship plowed its foamy way through the foggy North Sea, Elvis said, "Charlie, you keep me from going crazy."

The ship's officers kept the other soldiers busy sweeping

Feeling close on
the troop train...

Me 'n Elvis
and Ski...
Sailing for
Germany...

off the decks and scraping all the rusty spots off the iron.

They asked me and Elvis to put together some entertainment for the troops during the voyage. A sailor named Ski was in charge of production.

We spent a lot of time in Ski's compartment. He had his place fixed up nicer than most. He had an accordion lying around. He said he played it when he got lonesome. One day Elvis picked it up. He began playing it.

From out of the blue, a Navy photographer appeared. He got his Elvis picture. It showed Elvis looking up in surprise.

"Who the hell was that?" Elvis asked.

The photographer had vanished with his rare picture of Elvis playing an accordion. It would be worth a fortune if it could be found.

We put up notes on all the bulletin boards, asking anybody with any sort of talent to jump in and be part of the shows.

Elvis agreed to play the piano. "I'll be one of the backup musicians," he said. He didn't sing a single note. It must have been the only time in his life that he was on stage and never got introduced. But all eyes were on him. Magic was all around him.

Ski begged Elvis to just walk out on stage.

"Let's make this their show, not my show," Elvis said. "Let me just sit here and play piano for the performers."

Few entertainers ever had such an expensive man on piano.

Elvis got a kick out of how the ship's crew found a way to bring me a brew every day. They smuggled it in during rehearsals. It came in innocent looking soda pop bottles that the sailors had emptied - and then refilled with the good stuff.

"Charlie, you always figure out a way to get what you want," Elvis said one day as I sipped from the pop bottle.

I smiled, "I try Elvis."

He moved over a little bit on the piano bench.

"Sit down and play me something," he said. "A song we can harmonize on."

He nodded and smiled when my fingers picked out the first melodious string of notes in the gospel song, "His Hand In Mine."

That was a song we harmonized on for the rest of the trip and all the many months we spent in Germany.

They kept Elvis and us in quarantine for three weeks after we got off the boat in Germany.

His base was at Friedberg. Mine was 10 miles away at Kirch-Gons.

That part of Germany has a lot of beautiful old resort hotels. They attract mostly older people. They are real quiet. One of the best was the Park Hotel at Bad Nauheim. It was only a few miles from Elvis' base. The Park Hotel was where Elvis moved a couple of his employees and his father, Vernon, and his grandmother, Minnie Mae, whom he affectionately nicknamed Dodger. The rest of us called her Grandma.

On my first day off duty, I went by the Park Hotel and called Elvis' suite from the lobby.

Lamar Fike picked up the phone upstairs. He didn't know who I was.

"Charlie Hodge?" he said.

Elvis, deeper in the suite, yelled out, "Charlie! Get on up here."

Elvis came over to the door and hugged me when I walked in. He always loved to hug people.

He took me around the suite, introducing me to his people from Memphis.

"Tell Daddy some of the jokes you told me on the *Randall* coming over here," Elvis said. "Man, I don't know what I'd done without someone around to make me laugh, once in a while. Listen to this, Daddy."

So, Elvis put me to work making everybody laugh—the kind of job I had been working at for years, ever since I was a kid in Decatur, Alabama.

Grandma was bustling with joy when she came in.

"Dinner is ready, boys," she said.

Germany was the best thing that had happened to her in years. Back at Graceland in Memphis she had servants that waited on her, hand and foot. She didn't feel needed. But here in Bad Nauheim she was needed again. She was running the kitchen and feeding a bunch of hungry people. They all depended on her.

Elvis put an arm around my shoulder. "I'm just going to ask you once to eat with us," he said. "From now on, when it's time to eat, just come on in and sit down with the rest of us."

It was a royal welcome.

For the next year and a half, many of my weekends were warmed by the hospitality of Elvis at home.

One night at my base at Kirch-Gons, a corporal stuck his head in the door of my barracks and said they were holding a call for me from over at Bad Nauheim.

It was Lamar.

"Elvis is going to Munich," he said. "Then on to Paris. We'll be gone 15 days and we're leaving tomorrow. Me and Rex Mansfield are going and Elvis wants you to go. How early can you be here?"

Just like that. A call from the palace.

"Well, Lamar, let me talk to my sergeant," I said. "You know, the Army may have its own plans for Charlie Hodge's next two weeks."

"You want Elvis to call somebody over at your base and fix it for you?" he said.

14

"Naw, let me see what they tell me, first, Lamar."

I had put together a band to play on weekends at officers and non-com clubs in that part of Germany. There were eight of us. We each got 10 dollars a show. It was a little spending money.

The band was designed to give everybody what they wanted--an accordion to play the polkas always requested by visiting German officers, a cool trumpet to please the jazz fans, a steel guitar for Western swing buffs and a black boy who could play bluesy guitar. I emceed, sang, did voice imitations and a comedy spot.

When I wasn't doing the nightclub show, they put a little foot pump organ in the back of my Jeep and drove me around with the chaplains, all day on Sunday. I played spirituals and hymns at all kinds of church services in different styles.

I walked down the company street and found the sergeant.

He couldn't believe the luck I had. I was invited to spend a couple of weeks in Munich and Paris with Elvis Presley-- with Elvis picking up the tab on everything.

"Hell, yes, you can go," he said. "I just wish Elvis would ask me to come with him, sometime."

"Sarge," I said, "I'll put in a good word for you."

"Thanks, Hodge."

"Think nothing of it," I said.

I walked outside—then ran for a phone.

On A French Hillside
At Dawn . . .

In early morning darkness that had the smell of old dust, we rolled into the huge cavern of a train station in Paris. The great place echoed.

Freddy Beanstalk was waiting on the long platform for Elvis. He worked with Elvis' publishing companies that were operated by Hill & Range Publishing Co.

"Your first time in Paris, isn't it?" Freddy said.

Elvis nodded.

Freddy insisted that we first take a ride out into the surrounding hills.

"Elvis, you have to begin by seeing the sun come up over the city," Freddy said.

He said the edge of Paris was the best place for it. He took the wheel and drove us through the city and on out into the low hills of the countryside.

We parked and got out of the car and stood around in the cool dark. Waiting and yawning. Getting chilled.

Then the first glow of sunlight splashed pale yellow gold over the fantastic white dome of the Sacre Coeur Church. The Seine River turned into a winding rope of light. Sunlight turned the stained glass in Notre Dame Cathedral into a flickering fire of a thousand colors. You could imagine the ugly stone gargoyles on the cathedral hissing at the fire.

Freddy turned to Elvis. "Disappointed?"

"It's beautiful, Freddy," Elvis said. He winked at me. "They never had anything like this back in Tupelo."

Elvis remembered that sunrise all his life.

"On a French hillside at dawn—what a way to see the city of Paris for the first time," he often said.

The Prince de Galles Hotel at 33 Georg Cinq Avenue is two blocks away from the massive stone Arch of Triumph. Freddy got a suite for Elvis there.

I went for a quick walk as soon as we had checked in. I had to find a men's shop where I could buy a sport jacket and a white shirt and tie. I was sporting Continental threads

On the Champs Elysee
Elvis, Me and Rex...just before the fans hit...

when I came strolling back, my old Army uniform in a paper sack under my arm.

The grand old hotel looked like it was a castle under siege when I turned the corner a block away from it.

Elvis had hit Paris and the reporters came roaring in. It made you think of the stories of what it was like in Paris when Lindbergh landed there, years before.

There were a couple of hundred photographers and twice as many writers swarming through the lobby. Elvis had reluctantly agreed to give a press conference after Freddy Beanstalk pressed him.

Elvis' suite had the feeling of a barricaded fort. Elvis, himself, didn't seem all that bothered.

"You just have to be careful when you face these guys," he said, combing his hair at a wall mirror. "They need a story. That's how they make the money to pay for the rent and groceries. That is why I never really get mad at what they might say about me. They just have to dig for a living."

Rex Mansfield was from the little Tennessee town of Dresden. He wasn't quite ready for what happened in Paris. He tells it like this:

I had seen Elvis at press conferences before—when we were drafted together in Memphis and then down at Fort Hood when we all shipped out for Germany.

But this thing in Paris was what you would expect if the President of the United States showed up.

Everybody was packed and jammed into one of the huge lounges the hotel had. Television cameras and movie cameras were running like crazy. Flashes from hand cameras were blinding. Elvis was smiling and patient with everybody.

Me and the guys stood over against one wall, out of the way. Elvis sat behind a long table. About 25 microphones were bunched up in front of his face.

People were yelling all kinds of personal questions at him. They kept it up for two hours. Elvis got along with all of them beautifully. He was as calm as you please. Sometimes smiling. Sometimes joking with them. Sometimes so serious. Sometimes playful.

He seemed to know what mood was called for. He handled it like a great actor.

I had to keep pinching myself to make sure I wasn't dreaming all of this stuff.

Elvis seemed so much like one of us when he was off stage. In the spotlight, he seemed to turn into another person.

They loved Elvis. They kept telling him that Paris was accustomed to having big celebrities in town. They were used to seeing international stars walking along the boulevards. The reporters told Elvis not to worry—he could come and go in Paris with no problem. Fans in Paris would not be a problem. Mobbing Elvis was simply out of the question.

"I'm glad," Elvis said. "What I want to do is just wander around Paris like an ordinary person. Just relax."

No problem, they said. No one would pay him any mind.

Freddy Beanstalk finally called a halt to it and they let Elvis go back up to his suite.

"This is great," Elvis said when we got up there. He grabbed his hat and tugged it down at a little angle. "Let's us go out for a stroll."

We headed out the front door of the hotel behind Elvis.

Nothing happened. No big explosion. The people of Paris walked right around us.

We stopped at a little sidewalk cafe and sat down to do some girl watching.

A waiter came out on the sidewalk and brought us all a Coke with a slice of lemon in it.

"What do you call this?" Elvis asked the waiter.

"Coke *et citron*," the waiter said.

Elvis said, straight faced, "Just make my next one a Coke and lemon, please."

"*Oui, monsieur.*"

We laughed. The waiter looked pleased with himself.

Then we heard a kind of little scream. Female type. It was a kind of signal. In no time, hundreds of people were jammed around Elvis' table. Jabbering away with words you could only guess at. Finding paper in their bags and pieces of menus, anything, and asking Elvis to sign his name for them. Touching him. Giggling. Banging against his table. Spilling his drink.

We all jumped up and ran off down the sidewalk. We came to a movie house and went inside to get away from the crowd. We went straight on through and out the back exit.

We slipped back into the hotel and went upstairs to wait.

That night, late, we decided to try it again. Just to be on the safe side, we ordered a limousine. There would be no more luxury of strolling down the avenue.

"You guys can dress up casual. Any way you want to," Elvis said, studying himself in a long mirror hanging on the wall of one of the rooms of the suite. "I'm staying in my regulation dress uniform tonight."

We all looked up at Elvis and nodded. He knew he looked great in his uniform.

Elvis looked us all over when we got dressed. Then he gave each one of us a 100 dollar bill.

"You guys just use this for tips," he said. "I'll pay the bill." He paused. "And tip them heavy. We want to look good."

Every day in Paris, he gave each of us a 100 dollar bill just for tips.

The Twin Named Della . . .

The Lido nightclub is known around the world.

They have all kinds of acts going on. The place is like a big vaudeville show. People around you are speaking every language on earth, or seem to be.

The waiter put Elvis at a table right in front of the stage.

Elvis was intrigued immediately with one of the ice skaters who was a beautiful girl.

The rest of us only had eyes for all those pretty nude girls on stage.

I signed for this one for Rex when the cute Lido Club photographer brought it back that night. There's me, Rex, Lamar, a publishing company employee, and Elvis. Things picked up as soon as the waiters started filling up all those empty plates on the table.

The nudes were part of the visual entertainment but they never moved a muscle. They were unclothed mannequins. They posed, motionless as statues in a gallery. They framed the scenes on stage like Greek sculptures. Beautiful to behold. They looked like fine paintings borrowed from a big museum, miraculously brought to life. We didn't think they were vulgar in any way.

Two of the prettiest were twins from England.

Elvis said the twin named Della was the prettiest. I couldn't see much difference in them. Anywhere. Elvis began dating Della *and* the ice skater.

Both of the twins had beautiful eyes. Only Della had good vision. Della could see Elvis and the rest of us when we came in and took our usual table at the front of the stage. She was not supposed to move a muscle but she would smile at us, ever so faintly. Her sister's eyes would be searching the room for us and never see us.

Most of the nudes came over from England. They were no more than 15 or 16 years old. The management of the Lido would go over to London and make a deal with the parents of the most beautiful girls they could find. They brought them back to the club as mannequins while their bodies were fresh and firm and beautiful.

Each girl would be given to a French couple to live with. Even between shows the couple would come and collect the girls and take them back home until the next show. They really kept an eye on them. None of the natives or the tourists could take advantage of them.

The parents back in England were paid a good sum of money, as were their daughters. The couple in Paris who looked after the girls were paid a lot. They saw to it that no harm would come to the girls and they wouldn't go around with the wrong kind of man.

The Lido girls fell in love with Elvis.

Elvis would spend all night taking in the shows of Paris. At the Folies Bergere. The Moulin Rouge. The Carousel. The Cafe de Paris. The Lido.

22

They always let Elvis go backstage at the Lido. The show girls would gang around him. He'd invite them all to come along with us when we left after the last show.

Elvis always liked to spend the tag end of the night at a little place called Le Ban Tue. We called it the Four O'Clock Club. It opened its doors at four in the morning. Elvis always walked in at four-thirty with his string of beautiful show girls from the Lido—the Blue Belles.

Elvis liked to hang around the club until eight or nine in the morning and then take everybody back to his hotel. We'd get out of bed about eight the next night and start all over again—after a huge breakfast was brought up to us in the suite.

Early one evening, the Lido management called our suite for Elvis. They said they could not start the first show of the night until Elvis brought the Blue Belles back.

"I'll get them back right away, sir," Elvis said, smiling.

"Lamar, put the girls in limousines and send them off."

"They are beautiful," I said, standing at the window to watch them drive away.

Elvis smiled. "Thanks."

Elvis liked to kid you by taking credit for just about everything wonderful. If you went to the window in the morning and looked out and said, "Oh, what a beautiful morning," Elvis would look at you and grin and say, "Why, thanks, very much."

The weekend after our first trip to Paris, I got another call from Lamar.

"Elvis wants us all to go back to Paris," he said. "What have they got you doing over there?"

I went down to talk to the sergeant again.

He acted real nice.

Elvis drove us all to the station in his big Mercedes. Vernon came along to drive it back home.

The train to Paris had already left.

It was getting late in the day. An orange sun slipped down behind the old stone towers to the west of the station.

Elvis stood motionless on the empty platform.

He looked moodily down the tracks. A wind whipped at his jacket.

"Charter us a plane," he said.

Rex and Lamar got on public phones at the end of the platform. While Elvis paced back and forth, they yelled and pleaded with people. Finally, Lamar came trotting back.

"Elvis, we found a plane," he said. "But we can't find us a pilot."

Elvis glanced at his watch. He muttered something you would expect from an angry drill sergeant. Elvis cautioned everyone around him not to swear. He frowned on people taking the Lord's name in vain.

He walked over to the side of the tracks.

"Call that taxi driver, Joe," he said. "Tell him we have to go to Paris."

Lamar bounded down the platform to the phone booth again.

We ran down the steps of the station and out into the street. The cab was just turning the corner. Joe was fast.

We all jumped in.

"Paris," Elvis said. "Or catch the train that just went through here."

Joe grinned and gripped the wheel. The doors slammed shut. The cab made a mechanical roar. We took off down the highway like the lead tank in an invasion force.

The highway curved back and forth across the tracks of the railroad. After a while, we saw the twisting rear end of the train to Paris. It was headed toward a village in the distance. You could make out the church steeple and the low tower of the train station there. The driver swerved around a man on a bicycle in the highway. He pointed triumphantly to the train ahead.

Elvis nodded and grinned.

The row of windows on the waiting train looked like a gallery of pictures in iron frames. In one frame was an old man with a white moustache, smoking a pipe. In the next window was a girl with yellow hair and a soft smile. Beside her was a plain woman with no makeup and a handkerchief tied over her head. In another, a little boy, his nose pressed to the window. Two soldiers in American uniforms sat side by side in the next.

The train began moving again as we jumped out of the taxi.

Elvis never talked about wearing lifts in his boots so that he would look taller. We all wore lifts, especially me, but the subject was taboo.

Rex Mansfield didn't know not to talk about it.

"Where can I get some lifts in Paris?" he asked Freddy one night before we went to the Moulin Rouge.

We had come back to Paris and the De Galles Hotel.

Nobody answered him. We tried to simply ignore him.

"Where do you get your lifts, Freddy?" Rex repeated.

"What are you talking about, Rex?" Freddy asked vaguely.

"You know," Rex said, with a puzzled look. "Lifts! For your boots. Where can you buy them in Paris?" He looked at Elvis. "Elvis, where do you buy yours?"

Elvis' face was blank. "I don't know what you're talking about."

Rex frowned. He looked around the hotel room. He spotted Elvis' black boots at the end of the couch. He picked one up and dug out the lift in the heel.

"This is what I'm talking about, Elvis," he said. "Lifts! The kind you put in these boots."

With the Lido Club ice skater...

Elvis sighed and looked over at me. There was no way to avoid Rex now. Nowhere for Elvis to hide.

"Burnt," he said.

When somebody pinned you down on something you hoped to ignore, Elvis said you had been "burnt."

From the front door of the hotel you could walk down the noisy street a little ways and come out into the wide and beautiful Champs Elysee Boulevard. The Arch of Triumph was only a stone's throw away. On one corner, there, was a sidewalk cafe. Just across the boulevard was an entrance that led downstairs into the Lido. If you went straight on through the building you came out onto another street and Le Ban Tue nightclub.

Le Ban Tue was where Elvis liked to end his nights.

The little club didn't have much light. Elvis said the place was "intimate."

It was a place where many entertainers and dancers liked to go after the other clubs had closed and everyone was through working for the night.

It didn't have more than eight tables. Possibly nine.

"This place is no bigger than my living room back home at Graceland," Elvis said, looking around the place on the first night we went there.

We would sit around the club until daylight. Nobody but other entertainers around us. They all knew Elvis. They all liked him and tried to protect him from any kind of trouble.

The American newspaper columnist Dorothy Kilgallen heard that Elvis was in Paris one weekend. She found out he was coming to Le Ban Tue. She wanted to do an article on him. So she came to the club, sat down at a table near the door and waited.

It was a stakeout.

When Elvis finally arrived at the club, driving a Cadillac limousine he had rented, one of the girls sitting near the front door ran outside. She told Elvis not to come in unless, of course, he wanted to be interviewed by Dorothy Kilgallen.

"Go on inside," Elvis told us. "Let me drive around a little longer." He looked at the front entrance. "Maybe she'll go away after a while."

Me and Lamar and Rex climbed out and went inside and got a table. It was dark. Miss Kilgallen had no idea who we were. She looked at me once without any interest at all. Then her eyes drifted on.

Elvis drove back and forth along the Champs Elysee. Down to the Arch of Triumph and back again. Slowly. After a while, someone came out on the sidewalk in front of the club. When Elvis drove by, she flagged him to the curb. She said Miss Kilgallen had given up and left the club.

Elvis left the Cadillac at the curb and came in.

Usually when the people of Paris did recognize Elvis, they did try to leave him alone so he could relax and enjoy a bit of the normal life of the city.

One night we were standing outside the Lido. We were back in the shadows. Waiting for Rex to come on out so we could go on to Le Ban Tue.

A gentleman came strolling down the street. He saw us standing there in deep shadows. He paused. Then came over, creating a silhouette against the bright lights.

"Are you American soldiers?" he asked, with an accent I could not quite identify.

"That's right, sir," Elvis said.

The man paused. Then lit a cigarette. He had a slightly

theatrical face in the light of the small, bright flame.

"May I buy you a drink?" he said.

"I don't drink, sir," Elvis said.

The man shrugged slightly. "What's your name?"

"Elvis Presley, sir."

The man stood motionless a long time. He puffed on his cigarette. Then he flicked on his cigarette lighter and slowly held the little flame up to Elvis' face.

The flame clicked off.

"My God, you are Elvis Presley," he said.

A long limousine pulled up quietly at the curb behind him. Without another word, he turned and got in and the limousine disappeared in the night traffic.

One night one of the customers at another table came over to Elvis and whispered something in his ear.

"What was that all about?" I said as they turned and went back to their own table and sat down.

Elvis frowned. "I think what he said was that the GI sitting over there with that, uh, girl on his lap, really has a female impersonator on his lap—and doesn't seem to know it."

"What happens when he finds out?" I said.

Elvis shrugged. "I've been thinking about that."

A minute later, he got up and made his way through the shadows, between the squeezed tables, to where the GI sat with a dazed look on his face. The female impersonator on his lap looked up at Elvis and smiled.

"Hi, soldier," Elvis said. "I'm Elvis Presley."

The kid looked up at him, dumbfounded. Elvis bent down and whispered in his ear. The kid's eyes followed Elvis all the way back to our table. He hadn't said a word. In fact, he looked like he might have lost his voice permanently.

"What did you say to him?" I said.

"I just told him, 'Don't make a big scene, Chief, but your date is a femal impersonator,'" Elvis said, getting a piece of ice out of his glass. "I said, 'You've not got a girl sitting on your lap tonight.' I told him to wait a minute. Then tell his date that he had to go to the crapper. Then, just get the hell out."

In a minute, the soldier got up and headed for the toilet. He shot a glance at Elvis, going by, and touched the bill of his cap.

Elvis smiled.

After a while, the female impersonator got up gracefully from the table and drifted away into the night shades of Paris.

Elvis didn't have to go nightclubbing in Paris to have fun there.

One night, me and Elvis and Rex jumped in a taxi and headed for the Lido. We all felt good. We started singing. As we headed up the Champs Elysee it was just sparkling with night glitter.

When we were under the floodlit Arch of Triumph, Elvis leaned over the back of the front seat and told the taxi driver, "Turn around and drive us back down the street to the Eiffel Tower."

We kept on singing and harmonizing. All our favorite songs. "I'll Be Home Again." Some spirituals. Elvis kept telling the driver, "One more time. Up to the Arch and back."

When I looked at Elvis under the flickering lights I had the strange feeling that we had done this kind of thing at some other time. In some other life, maybe. I asked him about it later—when we were putting together his first Las Vegas stage show. His answer amazed me.

The
Summer
of '59...

...At Home...
at 14 Goethestrass

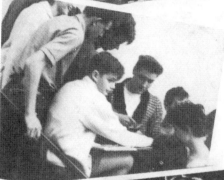

At the Front
Door...

...Singing with
Elisabeth...

Clowning in Khaki . . .

Cruising down the Champs Elysee, ours was probably the greatest backseat taxi trio in history with nobody around to enjoy it but the driver. I don't think we ever did get to the Lido that night.

Not far from Le Ban Tue was another little club that Elvis liked. It was called the Carousel. A couple of the boys who worked there always came to Le Ban Tue after finishing work at the Carousel where they did a female impersonator's act.

The two wore men's clothes while at Le Ban Tue but they still carried on like a couple of little old ladies.

One was named Alan. At the Carousel he was known professionally as Lana. He had created that stage name by moving the first letter of Alan down to the end of his name. That turned Alan into Lana.

One night we all dropped in the club. I took on a few drinks.

"The band sounds funny tonight," Elvis said.

"No bass," I said. "No bottom. Nothing but highs."

"You play bass?" Elvis said.

"Yea. A little."

The band's bass was leaning against the wall behind them. I put out my cigarette.

"Maybe they'll let me sit in," I said.

"Better ask them, first, if that's a French bass," Elvis said with a straight face. "I don't think you can handle it in *la francaise*."

I was up on the stage, playing. A beautiful blond girl looked up from a table nearest the band stand.

"Hi, there," she said.

The sound of a soft English voice in all the babel was a sweet one.

I smiled and almost lost the beat.

"Hello," I said.

"Do you recognize me, Charlie?" The voice was warm and wonderful.

I tried to focus my eyes better. I saw who it was!

"Alan! My God! You're beautiful," I said.

Elvis had been watching me and he nearly fell out of his chair, laughing.

Those people didn't upset Elvis. If Alan or his gay friends at Le Ban Tue had ever approached us, however, Elvis would have decked them.

One weekend Della came to Bad Nauheim to visit Elvis. She stayed at the house with the family.

Della was a city girl. She was absolutely thrilled by the quaint German countryside. She was enthralled by all the grazing horses and she wanted to go riding.

"Elvis, let's do go riding," she said. "Please, Elvis."

"I can't do it, honey," Elvis said. "That mob that hangs around outside this place would come after us on their own horses. We'd never get away from them.

"Charlie, can you take the lady riding?"

"Sure."

I didn't mind at all. I had developed a crush on Della.

I wasn't too good at riding. Della wasn't either, as it turned out. Her horse threw her when it first broke into a lope.

"Oh, my God," I said, jumping down to help her get up off the grass. Her hair was all messed up and cute. "I hope they don't have a newspaper photographer watching us behind those trees over there. They'll be blaming me tomorrow for killing Elvis Presley's girlfriend."

I wondered if she was going to show any bruises at her next show at the Lido.

They would have been hard to hide.

Elvis, driving a "Star" tank, gives his father and Elisabeth a
ride in Friedberg.

Elisabeth Stefaniak And
Grandma Presley . . .

Elvis had only one girl come live with his family at the three-story stucco house at 14 Goethestrasse in the old health spa of Bad Nauheim.

She was Elisabeth Stefaniak.

Elisabeth was of German stock. She had come to the United States after her mother had married an American career soldier stationed in Germany. During Elisabeth's senior year in an American high school, she returned to Germany when her American stepfather was ordered back and assigned to duty at Grafenwohr.

One night, she was hanging out in the lobby of an Army post movie house. Elvis and the guys were taking in a show there. She was hoping to catch a glimpse of him when he came out.

Rex came out to the lobby to buy Elvis some popcorn. He saw Elisabeth standing there. He invited her to come inside and join them.

That was the beginning of a real triangle.

Elvis let Elisabeth sit by him for the rest of the movie.

Elvis liked Elisabeth. She was pretty. She could speak both German and English. He quickly hired her onto his staff to move into 14 Goethestrasse to handle all his fan mail.

"She'd be good company to Dodger, too," Elvis said, meaning his grandmother who, until then, had been the only woman there except the landlady.

Elisabeth moved into her own private room upstairs.

Everybody instantly took a liking to Elisabeth.

The guys learned to depend on her. They even went to her for bar money.

Elisabeth tells how she got "truck driver wages" when she first moved in--and why:

Elvis' dad, Mr. Vernon, gave me $35 a week, plus room and board.

Everyone seemed to get that when they first came to work for Elvis. It must have had something to do with the fact that $35 was what they paid Elvis when he first went to work driving for Crown Electric in Memphis.

Out of that amount, I always had to loan Lamar and Red West a couple of dollars. They were not on Elvis' payroll but Mr. Vernon gave them both two dollars a week for spending money. Red was Elvis' oldest companion.

Red and Lamar would come to me at night for money so they could go down to Becks Beer Bar in Bad Nauheim and drink awhile.

Elvis wanted breakfast at home before going off to his Army work. So everyone living at 14 Goethestrasse but the landlady had to get up with him at five o'clock in the morning.

It would still be dark outside.

Lamar and Red would sit and yawn and shine Elvis' boots. Grandma would get his breakfast ready.

She always came in the kitchen with a wooden toothpick in her mouth. She was a very clean lady. Just spotless in everything.

She and I loved to talk quietly together in those early morning hours in the kitchen while we were busy getting Elvis' breakfast fixed.

I felt like a daughter and she treated me that way. We grew to really love one another.

Grandma taught me to cook breakfast the way Elvis wanted it. That way, if she got sick, I could do it for her. We always had crispy burned bacon, eggs flipped over hard because Elvis didn't like a runny yellow, and sliced peaches, butter and jelly and hot biscuits.

But when Elvis gained an ounce, the world just stopped until he could lose it.

Elvis left the house by six o'clock. Then I turned to opening the stacks of fan mail.

I think it was the beautiful gold crosses that the fans sent Elvis that impressed me most. Several gold crosses came in Elvis' mail each week. I put them all in a cardboard box.

Every day, Elvis got a letter from a very strange woman. It would describe a fantasy visit from Elvis during the night before. She would describe all the wildly passionate details of what had gone on between them.

Each weekend, she sent Elvis a big box of cookies.

"I'm afraid to eat them," Elvis said.

I threw them all out.

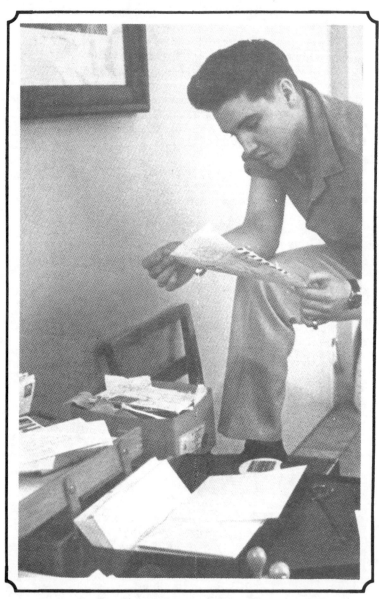

Reading a Letter from a Fan...

When Elvis heard about Jurgen Seydel he immediately had to meet him. Seydel was a famous karate expert. Karate was a physical kind of art that caught Elvis' passionate enthusiasm.

Elvis sent for Seydel. He moved all the furniture out of the living room. On weekends, he and Seydel worked out for hours at a time.

Elvis also hired Seydel to give karate instructions to Rex. That way, Elvis had someone to practice with when Seydel was not there.

Elvis called Rex "my enemy" during the karate workouts.

Rex began to feel that Elvis was taking advantage of him. He said Seydel always was careful to give Elvis better instructions than he gave Rex so that Elvis would always have an edge.

Elvis was always trying to be the best at everything he took up. Always studying. Few people would ever work as long and hard as Elvis did to perfect a thing.

Watching movies at the post movie house, he would be studying the actors. While I was simply enjoying the actors, he was studying them.

One day he said, "Charlie, screen lovers that last a long time in the movie business have what color hair?"

I shook my head. "I have no idea."

"Black," he said. "Charlie, you ought to start noticing such things. It all adds up."

Elvis' hair had been naturally light in his early movie, Love Me Tender.

It was dyed black for his later movies and stage concerts.

Elvis wanted his Jeep to be the best looking one in Germany.

When his reconnaissance battalion of the Third Army Division held a special inspection, Elvis got under his Jeep and sanded off the exhaust pipes.

He raised the hood and sanded his radiator. Some drivers painted their radiators black. Elvis' radiator shone like gold. When the inspecting officer raised the hood, it looked like Fort Knox.

"Sergeant Presley, this is the finest looking Jeep I ever inspected," the officer said, raising up.

Elvis beamed.

Elvis liked the military service. One day he told me, "If I weren't an entertainer already, I'd stay on in the Army."

He had been a member of the Reserve Officers Training Corps while in high school.

He had memorized Gen. Douglas MacArthur's famous farewell speech before a joint session of Congress after President Harry Truman had recalled him from Korea. He recited the speech in dramatic fashion. And he loved the movie MacArthur.

The character of Gen. George Patton fascinated Elvis. Time and again, we sat with Elvis at Graceland for still another showing of the movie, Patton.

The snow had been falling for several days at Grafenwohr where we played our war games.

Our sergeant came into my barracks one night. He came over to where we were all hunched around the stove. I was a Scout with the 15th Cavalry.

The sergeant knocked the snow off his thick shoulders. He unfolded a terrain map and spread it out on the bare floor.

He pointed to the maneuvers area.

I looked out the window at snow slanting through the yellow streak of light. It was drifting deep in places.

"Hodge," the sergeant was saying, "you'll take your Jeep and escort a gasoline tanker. You'll rendezvous with our forces at a bombed out church. Right here. Members of our own C Company will act as 'the enemy.' Avoid them at all costs."

The sergeant would not have been happy with what happened to me on maneuvers but it was enough to give Elvis a laugh when I told him about it a few nights later.

We were walking over to the army base theater and he asked me how the maneuvers went.

"You won't believe this," I said.

"When this big gas tanker followed my Jeep into the square in front of the old church, I looked around. 'The enemy' was standing all around us."

Elvis laughed. "You just drove right into the middle of them?"

"Yea. So I figured I had to try a big bluff on them," I said. "I stopped and got out of the Jeep and very calmly began directing the driver of the tanker, to help him back it up under some trees. Out of sight of any planes that might be scouting the area"

'Then I got back in the Jeep and drove it up under the foundation of the old wrecked church."

"They were watching me all the time. Then one of them eased up behind me and stuck his gun through the window behind me. A nice looking boy. Fair skin. Innocent blue eyes. Kansas wheat hair. He had the gold bars of a lieutenant on his shoulders. Maybe not long out of West Point.

"'You are my prisoner, soldier,' he said.

"I stared back at him as hard as I could. I shoved my cap down a little lower over my eyes. Kept chewing my gum. "'Sir, I'm not in the war games,' I told him. 'I'm supposed to bring this tanker out here and give Headquarters Company some fuel and then lead them back into camp.'

"He looked at me, like he was trying to figure me out, and then he said, 'Oh, I didn't know.'

"'No problem,' I said.

"He started to walk off through the falling snow. I called out, 'Sir!' "

Elvis shook his head. "You actually called the guy back after you once got away with it?"

I nodded. "The guy came back and I said, 'Would you happen to have any C rations? They didn't give us any before we left to come out here.'

"He dug a couple out of his pack and tossed them to me and went on off.

"Well, I got out of the Jeep and crawled up further under the old church flooring. I built me a little fire to get warm. Scooped up some snow in my metal drinking cup and put it on the fire. When it steamed, I made coffee with a little powder and wrapped my fingers around the cup to get them warm.

I rested my back against the cold stone foundation. Every once in a while I'd throw another little stick on the fire. Sip my coffee. Hum a little song. It wasn't so bad, once you got used to it.

It got to be 10 o'clock at night. I mean it got bone cold. Nobody ever did come for gas. The tanker just sat out there in the snowfall, getting covered up.

We drove back to the base around midnight.

My lieutenant was writing up a report when I got back. I told him how I talked the young lieutenant out of taking me prisoner. He laughed.

"There ought to be some kind of special medal for guys like you, Hodge," he said.

Elvis went out on maneuvers just a few weeks before he left Germany and it almost led to his death.

He told us about it when he came back in. We stood around in the living room at his house in Bad Nauheim, with a sick feeling in the pit of our stomachs while he told us about it.

"Charlie," he said, "shut the door so Dodger won't hear this. I don't want her to know anything about it. She'd die."

I shut the door and he told us.

"Me and my sergeant were out scouting this one area," he said. "I was driving.

"We got to this place and the sarge looked all around and said, "'Presley, we're in the Russian occupied territory. We'd better get the hell out. Think of the international incident they'd like to make out of this if they caught you driving around over on this side of the line.'

"Anyway . . . it started getting dark on us. We stopped at what looked like a safe place to sleep for the night.

"I left the engine running to get the heat off the exhaust pipes. That snow out there was up to your chin.

"We got our ponchos and pulled them up over our heads. Like a couple of tents, to keep the wind off us.

"Both of us went right to sleep. Then we started getting those gas fumes up under the ponchos. The next thing I knew, the wind blew one corner of my poncho away from my face. The fresh air woke me up some. That air had a kind of sick, sweet smell to it.

I was too sick and weak to even raise my hands. They just lay there in my lap. So I tried to tilt myself over and just fall out of the Jeep. I fell face down in the snow and got sick all over the place.

"I rolled over and looked back up at the Jeep. The sergeant was still sitting in it under his poncho. Sitting straight up. Stiff. Head down. He looked dead.

"I grabbed hold of a fender and pulled myself up on my feet. I just sort of stumbled against the sergeant's shoulder. He fell out of the Jeep in the snow on the other side.

"In a few minutes, he came to. I got him up on his feet.

"The Jeep engine was still running. Well, we got back in and took off. We decided not to tell anybody because it could get us both in trouble.

"So, don't you guys tell anybody.

"But that one was real close. Real close."

He signalled me to open the door again.

Only six weeks before Elvis left Germany, Priscilla Beaulieu walked through the front door of 14 Goethestrasse on the arm of Airman Currie Grant. The Airman managed the Eagle Club in Wiesbaden where Priscilla lived.

Priscilla instantly became the grand passion of Elvis' life. Everything and everybody else slid into the background of his life.

"She is everything I ever wanted," Elvis mused one night as he walked me out to the car that I was taking to pick Priscilla up for an evening with Elvis and his family.

Rex describes the incredible change that Priscilla brought in with her:

Elvis looked dazed. He lost interest in other girls around him. He seemed no longer aware of Elisabeth.

Grandma, of course, didn't feel very good about Elisabeth suddenly being forgotten. She was Grandma's favorite. If Grandma could have picked the girl for Elvis, it would have been Elisabeth.

There were so many charming things about Elisabeth. She had a way of dropping her eyes when you talked to her. She blushed easily, something that few girls do anymore.

Grandma was so upset, seeing Elisabeth unhappy, that she did something dangerous. She promoted a "forbidden romance" for her. She started telling me, "Rex, you know, Elisabeth will make some lucky boy a fine wife, someday." At the same time, she would go around to Elisabeth and say, "Rex is going to make some lucky girl a fine husband."

Somehow, Elisabeth and I began meeting quietly. First at the home of a friendly sergeant and his wife.

In the evenings, after supper, Elisabeth would tell Elvis, "Well, I think I will go visit Dee Harris a little while tonight." I would already be over at Sgt. Harris' house, waiting for her to come.

It scared me to death.

Elvis had a sensitive ego. If he had found out that his own grandmother was helping me and Elisabeth get together, he would have felt betrayed. He would have kicked me out of the house. Grandma would have been in a lot of trouble, too.

"You two children be careful," she kept whispering to us.

I met Lamar one night over at the Park Hotel to discuss the whole situation.

It was strange. Everybody in the house was aware of it. Everybody but Elvis. For some reason he had not found out. I think it was because he was so fascinated with Priscilla that he couldn't see anything else going around around him.

My own personal hell was that I knew Elisabeth would try to hang onto Elvis as long as she felt she had the slightest chance to get him for herself.

Elvis told me, over and over, "Charlie, Priscilla is the most beautiful creature I ever saw."

Priscilla did have a way about her, when she was around Elvis, that made her seem far older than her 14 years. She had a kind of poise. An aloofness about her. She had an ethereal little smile that made her seem like a cosmic princess from some other world.

"Like an angel," Elvis explained, simply.

There was no doubt that Elvis wanted her to follow him back to Graceland when his tour ended and he got on a plane to fly home.

Everybody at 14 Goethestrasse wanted to move to Graceland with Elvis. There was a magic around him. Nobody wanted it to end.

But something was bound to end for Elisabeth and Rex, the moment we got back to Memphis.

Rex told me later, how it all came down:

Elisabeth rode back to Memphis on the train with Elvis. She still hoped he would prefer her to all the girls who were gathering around him.

One day, though, Elvis told her quietly that his restriction on her dating anyone else was now lifted. He said it would be all right if she dated some of the guys.

When she told me what he had said, I decided to go in and tell him that I intended to marry her.

45

He was putting on a formal outfit. Standing in front of the mirror. He said he was taking a group to the movies.

"You want to go along with us?" he said.

"I'm really more interested in taking Elisabeth out," I said.

He looked at me through the mirror. He was combing his hair. After a minute, he said, "Go ahead, Rexodus. It's fine with me."

For some reason, I was unable to bring up the subject of marriage.

Elisabeth still delayed making a decision between us. I decided to turn cold on her. Maybe that would force her to make some kind of choice.

It worked. She cried.

A few days later, she told Elvis she wanted to go down to Florida to visit some relatives.

As soon as she left the mansion, someone told Elvis she was meeting me.

"They're running off to get married," he told Elvis.

Elvis came running out of the mansion after her.

He caught her and said, "Are you meeting Rex?"

"No, Elvis," she said. "I'm going to Florida to visit my relatives."

He stood there a minute, looking at her. Then he nodded. "It's all right. Go on."

Elvis never saw Elisabeth or Rex again. They got married in Rex's home town but never returned to Graceland.

From that day on, Elvis thought only of Priscilla.

After I got out of the Army I took a train down to Decatur to see my folks.

They looked at me with unbelieving eyes when I told them about life in Europe with Elvis Presley.

It did sound unbelievable. Even to me.

Something pulled me back to Graceland. Like a magnet. When I walked in, everybody was getting ready to go to

At Army farewell, Elvis and Rex ponder future...

Nashville. Elvis was going to record his first album since coming home from Germany. It was to be titled, "Elvis is Back."

"You want to go up to Nashville with us?" Elvis said. "I chartered a bus so everybody can go."

"What would I do up in Nashville all that time?" I said. "I don't know."

"How about recording 'I Will Be Home Again' with me — a duet like we did on the *Randall*, he said. "That'd be the first full duet I ever put on an album."

"Are you kidding me?" I said.

He grinned. "Get on the bus and see," he said.

Elvis had to break off the Nashville recording sessions long enough to go to Miami to do a show with Frank Sinatra. He had been out of the Army only one month. Miami was to be his first public appearance as an entertainer in a long, long time. But, then, he was always a bit nervous before walking out in front of an audience. He was nervous through the Las Vegas years and on all the big tours.

Once on stage however, he had the confidence of Allah.

When he got back from the Sinatra show he told the crew that we were going to record "I Will Be Home Again" and it was going to be the next one done.

I had found a recording of it on a Golden Gate jubilee spiritual album in a Post Exchange in Germany. I bought it and gave it to Elvis the next time I went over to Bad Nauheim.

He loved the whole album.

Elvis started telling the studio musicians how we had sung it a lot, sitting around the barracks in Germany.

"There were a lot of lonesome boys over there," he said. "It would almost make them cry."

Elvis, on the bus ride back to Memphis, talked about going to Hollywood to do a new movie which Col. Tom Parker had arranged for him. It was GI Blues.

"The Colonel got a suite for us on the sixth floor of the Beverly Wilshire Hotel," he said. "Some of you guys will stay up in the penthouse. I'll come up there and lie around whenever I want to get some sun tan."

The Colonel had hired two railroad cars for Elvis and all the guys. The trip to the West Coast was going to be a ball.

One car was a sleeping car. It had private compartments for Elvis, the Colonel and everybody. The other car was a combination dining car and lounge.

The colonel had an amusing way of dealing with all the big shots and the movie moguls who came to see him even before the train could pull out of Memphis.

They would come rushing up to him and say, "Colonel, I have to talk to you."

He'd nod and get up and open the door to the bathroom and say, "Step right in my office."

Maybe it was his sense of humor. Or maybe the toilet was a good place to talk privately with someone, where nobody would interrupt them. I don't know what the reason was— but it was a habit Elvis picked up later on. I remember that Richard Davis said one night in Hollywood that Elvis had him step into his toilet—talked things over and then offered him a job as one of his personal valets and body guards. A job that he grabbed.

Elvis stood on the steps of the lounge car, looking down the platform. They were waiting for some of his folks to get there. Then they would roll out.

Everybody around him was talking about things coming up for them on the West coast. It sounded like dream time.

I kept thinking about things that we had done together in Paris and Frankfort and Bad Nauheim.

I listened to all the bubbly talk that people make when they are on the verge of leaving on a fabulous trip. It me feel even lonlier.

I was at loose ends.

After Elvis' train left, I was going to ride back out the Graceland with Vernon to get my clothes and then head back to Decatur.

Elvis looked down at me from the steps of the lounge car.

"Charlie," he said.

"Yea, Elvis?"

"You want to climb on? Go to Hollywood with me?" he said.

"How could I just climb on?" I said. "I don't even have any clothes with me. They're all back at Graceland."

"What do you want clothes for?" Elvis said. "Get yourself some new stuff on the Coast."

He looked down the platform.

"Better decide quick," he said. "I'm going to let this train roll out of here."

I didn't wait. I crawled on.

Incredible Journey . . .

Thus began an incredible journey.

People were gathered at every little train station and crossroads out in the country to see Elvis' train go by. They had heard he was back home and was going to Hollywood to make a movie.

They wanted to see him. It was historic to them. They were out there standing alongside the tracks, no matter what time of the day or night you pushed the curtain aside and looked out the window. There could be as many as 50 people at nothing more than a whistle stop on the empty plains.

They would wave and smile. They yelled words of encouragement to Elvis. Some wiped away tears. Some brought their babies to hold up in the air for Elvis to see. It all made you wonder.

Elvis got very quiet whenever he looked out.

It was sort of like the old days in America when politicians travelled around the country on their private campaign trains. They would stop and make speeches from the platform of the observation car at the tail end of the train. People would gather at all the little stations. They would run across the fields to every country crossroads to see them. It must have been like that even when Cleopatra floated down the broad Nile, her people watching her progress from the banks.

There is a Mystery...

There is a mystery to such things.

There was even a sort of mystery about my own life. At least, my father thought it was a big mystery. He saw how well I did and it baffled him.

My life trained me for a future with Elvis, right from the start.

It began with someone bouncing me on their lap on Saturday nights when the family sat in our living room in Decatur and listened to the radio program coming from the Grand Ole Opry in Nashville.

There was a comic on Roy Acuff's part of the show named Cousin Oswald. He had a peculiar laugh. One night, I imitated it. Everybody looked at me and laughed. That was the first laugh I got as an entertainer. I never got over it. I began imitating other famous people's voices. People kept laughing at me.

I picked up piano playing and guitar strumming in high school. I started singing tenor in the Sixteenth Avenue Baptist Church choir. Dad said that on summer nights, when they had the church windows open, you could hear my voice over everybody else's when you drove past.

Shorty Sullivan heard me one night. He hired me at five dollars a night to sing with his Green Valley Boys on WHOS radio. We played in school auditoriums. Shorty liked the way I could imitate Jimmy Dicken's voice singing, "Take An Old Cold Tater and Wait" and others like it.

Then the WHOS station manager, Louis Blizzard, saw

With a country front porch as my stage, a dollar uke to strum...with a watermelon for my chair...look out, world!

...and then, working with Gene Autry.

me working in the studio and asked if I would like to spin records on the air and read the prepared scripts on them.

Later, Blizzard let me add a gospel show with people calling in requests. Gospel singers were the biggest stars in the world to me. I was always hanging around backstage when the gospel shows played my home town. The singers would stop by and talk to me, pat me on the shoulder and autograph their albums for me. They would tell me little stories I could pass along to my radio listeners.

It made me a celebrity around Decatur.

When Elvis Presley later said for me to find him a good gospel quartet for his road show, I knew who to pick up the phone and call. They were my friends.

All of the little parts of my musical life then seemed random and haphazard. But they all came together and fell into place, later on, as if there was a master plan from the beginning.

There was a man living in Decatur named Griggs. He got together with his two daughters to form a vocal trio. They did pretty well until Griggs walked out on the girls and joined the Decatur Stamps Quartet.

"I think I'll see if I can take Mr. Griggs' place with his two daughters," I said one night at supper.

Dad eyed me and wiped his plate with a piece of bread.

"Charlie," he said, "they're not going to want a boy like you. They are professionals. You never did anything like that. Sitting in a church choir is one thing. Imitating Jimmy Dickens is another. But this is something else entirely. I would hate to see you disappointed."

I nodded. "Me, too."

The two girls had an audition set up the next day for someone to take their father's place in the trio.

I'll do anything for a laugh...
in 1952.

I tried out. When I finished, I walked over to the oldest one of the sisters. She looked like she might be turning into the boss.

"Do I get the chance, Robbie Jean?" I asked.

We soon became the hottest thing in North Alabama. We worked at all-day singings and dinners on the ground at churches all over that part of the South.

One night, Robbie Jean's sister, Claudelle, said, "Daddy left the Decatur Stamps Quartet last night. He left town."

I mentioned it at supper that night.

I listened to Dad's knife sawing away on a piece of meat in his plate. Then he cleared his throat.

"Charlie, the Decatur Stamps are real professionals," he said. "All grown men. Accomplished in music. They simply can't use a boy like you. It just wouldn't look too good."

I got the job.

Three nights after high school graduation, Willard Lake and his wife, Jewel, drove up to the curb in front of our house. They were driving to Dallas and offered to take me with them. I wanted to go study at the Stamps Quartet School of Music in Dallas.

"Riding with them will save you train fare," Dad said.

We hugged each other and Mother tried not to cry. Then I was gone.

A lot of boys came in from the countryside. Bill Gaither came down from Indiana. Right off, we knew we wanted to work together if we could. But after school was over Bill got on a train and went back home to Indiana.

I found a bass singer in Decatur and we went up to Indiana and put together a quartet, with me singing baritone.

We sang in little churches and auditoriums all over Indiana and Ohio. Somehow, we got down into Florida and that was where things came apart. The string of dates ran out. We couldn't even find a place to sing for our supper.

Bill and I went back to Indiana and put together another quartet with me singing high tenor. We called ourselves the

Pathfinders. We landed a radio slot on WRFD in Worthington, Ohio and we moved into a little hotel in a little town not far away called Delaware. There was a little coffee shop down at the end of the street. We'd go down there and drink coffee and dream.

The beautiful former wife of our lead singer showed up on the front row of one of our concerts one night. She was in a blue dress with a lacy collar. After the show, she came backstage. She smelled of lavendar and roses. She told the guy that, if he would get off the road, she would marry him again. He looked at her and couldn't resist. He never had been able to resist. He told us we had to find us a new lead.

Then the wife of the bass singer told him she was going to leave him if he didn't get "a real job."

Bill watched the cracks widening in the group and he said, "Oh, well. I always did want to go to college more than anything."

They were going to leave me alone out there on stage. Singing high tenor.

I was moping in the dressing room of a little high school one night. We had done our spot on the show. The other guys had gone on to a restaurant. I was to catch up if I felt like it. Some other quartet was singing on the high school stage.

I heard the lowest rumble in human creation.

"Don't I know you, son?" it said.

I turned with a big grin.

It had to be J.D. Sumner, the one man that God had given the longest vocal chords that He had ever made. At least, that's what I used to tell my radio listeners back in Decatur when I had a gospel record program.

"I'm on the show tonight with the Sunshine Boys, coming up next," he rumbled, running a white comb through his hair at the mirror.

He stuck the comb in his back pocket. "But I'll tell you, Charlie, if they don't start making some real money, soon, I'm taking an offer I just got from the Blackwood Brothers.

The Blackwoods want me. Bad. And they've got the money."

He checked his hair one final time in the mirror, ran an open palm over it and then hit me with his brightest stage smile.

"See you, kid."

It was a prophecy. In time, we would see each other every night across Elvis' stage.

Late that night, I was sitting by myself in the little coffee shop just down the street from our hotel in Delaware.

A waitress with dyed yellow hair like straw was being real nice to me. It was late. Near closing time. I could feel that she was drawn to me.

She bent down to fill my cup and smiled straight into my eyes.

"Anything else tonight?" She toyed with her hair.

I shook my head. "Say, I'm with the Pathfinders. We're in a gospel concert tomorrow night at the church over there. Won't you come? I know it would be a blessing to you."

I beamed my brightest.

She straightened and laid a thin, stony smile on me.

"Well, I'm just afraid I have to work," she said.

She dumped my ashtray and went back behind the counter. She shot a look up at the clock behind the cash register.

"We'll be closing in three minutes," she said briskly.

I got up and paid. "If you change your mind . . ."

She looked at me and bit her lip to keep from saying something she might regret. "I'll pray about it," she said.

When the quartet sank beneath the waves, I took a bus back to Decatur and got a cab out to the house.

The folks didn't bother me with a lot of questions. They let me sleep late for several days.

One night at supper, Dad cleared his throat and said, "Son, what are your plans?"

"Well, I think I'll go to Detroit. I have friends up there. Maybe I'll get a job making cars."

"It'd be honest," he said.

When I got to Detroit, I went out to see my friends. When I walked in the door they said Frank Stamps had called from his company headquarters in Dallas. He was the president.

I called him right back.

"There's a group in Shenandoah, Iowa that needs a good baritone," he said. "They'll pay 50 dollars a week to start. I'll call them and tell them you're coming. Good luck, Charlie."

I put down the phone, picked up my suitcase again and was on the next train to Shenandoah.

Only three weeks later, we were singing on the same bill with one of the nation's top gospel groups, The Foggy River Boys, in a concert in a little town in Iowa. The Foggies backed Red Foley on his Ozark Jubilee, a weekly ABC television network show from the stage of the Jewel Theater in Springfield, Missouri.

After the concert we all went across the street to a cafe to get something to eat. We felt good.

The Foggies' manager, Bill Matthews, caught my eye across the table. He signalled me to come outside on the sidewalk with him.

Outside, he said, "Charlie, how about joining the Foggies? Our lead singer is leaving us. You can fill it. We liked the way you worked tonight. Getting laughs. Holding it together. What do you say?"

It was sort of abrupt. I had been with my group only a few days, really.

"Let me think about it, Bill," I said.

"Don't take too long," he said. "We have to fill the spot."

I told my guys what Bill had offered me.

"There would be a lot more than 50 dollars a week in it," I said. "And they are getting regular weekly network television exposure. What should I do?"

The business manager just threw up his hands.

"Just go," he said.

I felt like apologizing.

Standing on my crate . . .

The Foggy River Boys always ran out on stage to begin their show.

I started carrying an empty Coke case out on stage with me to stand on. I was only five feet and three inches tall.

The other guys towered over me if I didn't have something to stand on top of.

The Coke case gave the audience a reason to chuckle. It had them on my side from the start.

And that was the way Elvis and his cousin, Billy, saw me singing on the Ozark Jubilee show at the auditorium in Memphis, just before we both were drafted.

Elvis saw me standing on an old crate, singing. The memory always gave him a chuckle. And Elvis liked to have people around him who knew how to bring a chuckle to the world.

"Every great person in history has had a kind of court jester, or a comedian, around him," Elvis told me once. "He's always had someone who can make him laugh.

"The comic can get away with saying just about anything to him—and he can say anything he wants to his jester and the guy won't get mad at him."

That was to be part of my job for Elvis.

A Bedraggled Little Girl...

Hollywood was drawn to Elvis when his special railroad cars rolled into town after he came home from Germany.

They all came. Old movie stars. Young television actors. People who claimed they were Elvis' distant relatives. Fans from Kansas. Hucksters. Investment counselors.

All of them were dreamers, in all the varied forms that they can assume. Each had his own private dream. Each saw Elvis Presley as the person who could make the dream come true.

Strangely, Elvis was drawn to a bedraggled little girl he saw in a corner of his crowded Beverly Wilshire Hotel suite at a welcoming party for him.

She looked like she had just climbed out of somebody's swimming pool a few minutes ago and didn't have time to get her hair dried good. And hadn't bothered with her clothes at all because she never dreamed she'd end up in Elvis Presley's private suite in Hollywood.

Her name was Lindalee Wakely. She was the beautiful child of Jimmy Wakely, a cowboy movie star and Nevada lounge circuit entertainer. Some called Wakely a "singing cowboy." He was far more than that and he became far more than that to Elvis.

This is how Lindalee saw Elvis arriving in Hollywood:

For me, it was a horrible scene. Just horrible. But Elvis turned it all around.

I did a Hollywood gossip column for a fan magazine called Teen Scene. You may remember it.

62

Well, Dad had know Elvis' manager, Col. Tom Parker, and his wife, Marie, for many years. So Dad was able to get me an interview with the great Elvis who had just come back from Germany and had come out to the West Coast to make movies.

The interview was going to take place on the set of GI Blues. It really was a fantastic break for a kid like me. I knew it. I bought new shoes. I chose a new dress. I got an appointment with an expensive hairdresser. I was shaking but I was going to look sharp and make a great impression on Elvis.

Saturday afternoon, before the interview, I dropped by a girlfriend's house. She used to work for Elvis a little and I wanted to ask her about him.

We decided to go swimming. We were out in her pool and she got a phone call. It was some of Elvis' people. They wanted her to come by and pick them up and all go out to the beach. She told them, "Give me half an hour."

She dressed to the hilt. Makeup. Cashmere sweater. High heels. The works. She said she would change back into a swim suit at the beach. Not to worry.

I had nothing to wear but what I came in.

Not to worry, she said.

We drove the back streets of Beverly Hills. We turned into the underground garage at the back of the hotel and took a rear elevator upstairs. We were just picking up some guys, then going on down to the beach.

When the elevator door opened, we were suddenly in a fabulous suite. Elvis was standing on the other side of the room in a crowd in front of a huge picture window. I nearly died. I stopped breathing. There were gorgeous women everywhere. Handsome men. Rafts of them.

I had on an old faded pair of stretch toreador pants. Not one touch of makeup anywhere. Hair still damp from the pool but a little curl coming back in it. And Dad's old corduroy shirt.

Then I remembered the worst. I was barefoot. No shoes.

I wedged my way through the crowd to a corner seat and sat down on my bare feet to cover them up. I tried to look like I didn't have a care. I hoped nobody in that mob would bother to give me a second look.

Then a little guy came over, neat and smiling.

"You're Jimmy Wakely's kid?" he said. He had a kind of nice Southern drawl.

"You know my Dad?" Who is this guy, I wondered.

"I'm Charlie Hodge," he said. "I sang with the Foggy River boys before me and Elvis went to Germany. Yea. I worked with your Dad on the Ozark Jubilee on ABC."

He sat down on the floor beside me and started chatting away. He was adorable. I just loved him. He made me feel like I was safe and at home there.

I actually was feeling like I would get away with it when I looked up and there was Elvis looking down at us with an amused smile.

"You sure look like kinfolks," Elvis said, eyeing my clothes. "Maybe like a cousin of mine."

I poked at my ropy hair. "Your cousin must be a real knockout."

"It's not a girl," he said. "It's a boy. Named Billy Smith. You two sure look alike."

Charlie jumped up. "This is Jimmy Wakely's little girl, Lindalee," he said.

It was not the way I planned to meet Elvis Presley at all. I wanted to cry.

Elvis winked. "Stand up and let me see your outfit, Lindalee," he said.

I got up and stood there, bare feet and all.

"Lindalee," he said, "you look like family to me. From now on, that's the way we're going to treat you anytime you come see us."

He patted my shoulder and walked on.

I was in a state of shock but it began to feel real good.

I was still feeling that crazy kind of high on Monday on my way to the interview. During a break in one of the dance sequences, Elvis ducked into a studio conference room to talk with me, to two other magazine writers and a photographer from Europe.

Afterwards, I remember his smile, mostly. He sent words weaving through my mind like strings of colored balloons in a bright blue sky. He really made you feel like that.

Then Elvis had to leave us to go back to the cameras. I walked dizzily back to my car in the parking lot. I already knew the title of my article. It would be called, "A Handful of Stars." It was from something my Dad once told me.

Dad said, "Lindalee, when you can walk down a street anywhere in the world and everybody turns and says, 'There's So-and-So,' then you know you are a great star.

"But in all the world, there are only a handful of stars."

When I got home and went in the house I felt an urge to do something nice for Elvis Presley. I went to the kitchen and mixed a batch of fudge. The next day, I took the fudge back to his hotel.

Elvis had finished shooting his picture. The guys were already packing his personal belongings for the trip home.

Elvis wanted to be home as soon as possible.

Elvis grabbed a piece of my fudge and bit off a chunk.

"What's this, little one?" he said.

"It's Oakie Fudge," I said.

'Oakie' is a nickname for an Oklahoman—my Dad was from Oklahoma.

"Oakie Fudge?" Elvis said.

"Yea. Just Plain Old Fudge," I said.

"It's just the kind I like," he said. He licked his fingers. "Little one, it's the best I ever ate in my life. Thanks."

I smiled in a kind of silent delirium and drifted back toward the elevator. When I punched the Down button, I felt like I went up.

The next day, I heard Dad tell Mom that he was having trouble finding a good tenor. He was putting together another one of his shows to take out on the Nevada circuit of saloons and gambling lounges. It was big money out there, stylish and sophisticated. Acts had to be tops. Nothing cornball allowed.

"Dad," I said, "I met a boy yesterday at Elvis' hotel who said he had worked with you on the Ozark Jubilee. His name is Charlie Hodge."

"Is he with Elvis now?" Dad asked.

"He was yesterday," I said.

Charlie worked in Dad's show for the next five years, 1961 to 1966, when he wasn't off making movies with Elvis.

Going Home . . .

One night, I came back in off the road with Jimmy.

The guys at Elvis' house on Perugia Way were loading his bus.

Elvis had just finished making a movie. He wanted to leave immediately for Graceland.

"Load up, Charlie," he yelled when I walked in.

"Have a heart," I said. "I just came off the road."

He grinned. "I said, put your clothes on the bus."

Elvis worked real hard when he was making a movie, or at anything else he was putting his mind to. But as soon as he finished, he just wanted to jump in his mobile home and get back to Memphis as soon as he could.

He found a lot of privacy out there when he was on his 1963 Dodge, crossing the countryside. He didn't have his name painted on the side of it like a lot of entertainers did. He kept it plain. Unmarked. He could stop anywhere and people wouldn't notice him until he was about to leave. Then he could go sign a few autographs for them and drive on.

Sometimes, late at night, he would pick up the CB microphone and call out, "KDD8876 Unit 1 to Unit 2. Find us a place for the night."

Some of the guys were in a station wagon trailing right behind Elvis' mobile home. They would hear his message and would pull out in front of us, flash their lights a couple of times and race ahead.

They kept a special book with the names and addresses of all the good motels on the roads we usually took. In summer, we usually took old Route 66. The winter route took us down through Dallas and Phoenix. When Elvis felt ready to turn in, the guys would get up ahead of us to the next town and get accommodations for all of us. It was all arranged by the time we rolled into town.

That way, Elvis could get in and out of a town quietly.

But Elvis usually liked to drive straight through the night.

One night, coming to Memphis from Hollywood in the mobile home, Elvis flipped across the radio dial and tuned in the George Klein show from Memphis.

Elvis liked George and he made sure George always got the first copy of any record he made.

That night, George put on one by Tom Jones singing, "Green, Green Grass of Home," a real nostalgic thing.

Elvis listened. His eyes glistened at the end of the song. He brushed a hand across them.

Elvis had been away from home a long time, making three movies. He was real homesick by the time he left Hollywood.

At some little town in Arkansas, all the streets were dark except for one bright light coming out of an outdoor phone booth. On a corner by a dark filling station. Elvis hit the brakes and swerved to a stop by the phone.

"Joe," he said, "jump down and go call George. Tell him to play it again."

Joe always carried Elvis' phone book so he would be able to get anyone Elvis wanted to talk to at any time, day or night.

"You mean 'Green, Green Grass of Home?' " Joe said.

Elvis nodded.

We all got quiet and listened while Tom sang and the mobile home rolled on east. The dark highway was almost empty at that time of the morning.

Elvis stopped every time we came to another outdoor phone booth. Joe jumped down and ran over to it and called George in Memphis.

"He wants to hear it again, George," Joe said, at the next stop.

"Did he say why?" George asked.

"No."

"Where are you now?" George asked.

"About 40 miles out," Joe said.

"Okay, you got it."

George must have played it eight or 10 times.

Joe jumped back in, just in time to hear George say on radio, "Now, one more time for the King. See you soon boys."

When the big tires hummed onto the bridge across the Mississippi River, Elvis pointed up at a thin slice of moon just over the horizon. It looked like it was hooked onto the side of the tall bank building.

Elvis began to slow down ever so slightly. And to relax.

If you listened, you could him humming softly, "Green, Green Grass of Home."

Home and the home fires were always big with Elvis.

Elvis loved to drive. He dressed special for it.

He would put on his big sun glasses. And tug on one of those narrow brimmed hats he had so many of. He had an incredible collection of hats and always travelled with a trunk full of them. Then he would pull on his special driving gloves. Next, he'd light up a long, slim cigar.

Then, Elvis was ready to roll.

He drove with one foot up on the dash of his mobile home.

He'd come barrelling across the desert out of California. He raced the big highway trucks along the way. Most of the truckers recognized Elvis when they came alongside him. They would wave and pull the rope on those big horns and get a big kick out of it all.

Elvis could entertain himself all day long, dueling with the big trucks on the highways.

He was playing the game to win, all the time.

Driving A Runaway . . .

I'm alive today because Elvis was at the wheel of the mobile home coming down the side of Big Bear Mountain in California. He was up there on location, shooting the film for Kissing Cousins.

When I came back from the Nevada circuit with Jimmy Wakely, the maid said Elvis was up around the ski resort at Big bear Lake. She said Connie Stevens was up there, dating Elvis.

I drove out toward Palm Springs. Took a left at San Bernardino. The road wound up into the mountains. A gorgeous drive. The air turned real fresh and clear as I came out on top of the mountain.

Sunshine was bouncing off Big Bear Lake in the distance. Elvis' mobile home sat under the shade trees around a house that the Colonel had rented for him to live in during the filming.

At first, I thought a soldier was walking toward me across the clearing. It was Joe Esposito, top man on Elvis' staff. Joe had a bit part as a soldier in one of the scenes that day.

On a trip to Paris, Joe started picking up and saving all of Elvis' expense receipts. Elvis asked what he was up to and Joe said, "You can use these on your income tax."

Elvis smiled. "Joe, I need you working for me—full time."

"You got up here to Bear Lake just in time," Joe told me. "Elvis is taking us all down to Palm Springs for the weekend."

The day the film crew got the last footage in the can, dark snow clouds came scooting over the top of the mountains. It started to mist and rain. Cameramen ran around, grabbing a few last background shots.

Elvis had already come back in and changed clothes.

It was getting dark with lots of heavy snow clouds rolling in.

"Hey, guys," Elvis said. "Let's hustle. this rain can turn to snow any minute now. We don't want to get caught in it up here. It'd be a week before we could get down off here."

The guys were running around, packing and loading up all the cars and the mobile home.

I flipped off the rest of the house lights and we ran for the mobile home.

"Charlie," Elvis said, "tell Chief to bring your car down the mountain. You're riding with me.

"I heard the man," Ray Sitton said when I tossed him the keys.

Ray was a huge guy. A good 300 pounds. As big as

Lamar. He made the springs sag when he plumped down in the seat of my Ford.

I jumped in the mobile home. Rear wheels tossed up gravel. Elvis swung out of the parking area and onto the road that dropped off down the mountain.

Darkness began filling the little valleys and hiding the sides of the hills.

After a few miles, Elvis said, "You guys better put on your seat belts." His eyes were on the road.

Joe, in the co-pilot's seat, glanced at him. "How come?"

"No brakes," Elvis said.

He slapped the brake pedal with a black boot. It went slack, almost to the floor.

"They're gone," he said.

He tried grinding the gear shift into reverse. It growled and trembled the mobile home for an instant and popped loose. We kept gaining speed.

Curves began coming so fast it scared me.

I sat on the engine hump between the two front seats.

Then the cold front hit us. The sky turned black. Sleet and icy rain slapped the windshield.

The dash lights went out. Then the windshield wipers stopped.

Elvis flipped the wiper controls. Nothing happened. A black boot hit the floppy brake pedal. Nothing.

The windshield wipers had stopped working halfway through their arc. They stood straight up. Sleet started building up on the glass between them. It was like trying to see through a frosted window. It was dark out there in front of us.

Joe rolled down the window on his side. He got a coat hanger out of a closet and reached and hooked it on the base of the windshield wiper on his side. He shoved it back and forth. It cleared a little patch to see through but sleet was covering Joe up like a snowman.

Joe's lips were moving. I leaned over and yelled, "What did you say, Joe?"

He yelled back over his shoulder, "I'm not talking to you. I'm praying!"

"Just don't stop," Elvis yelled at him, gripping the wheel.

We followed the headlights around the curves.

"If we meet a car coming up the mountain," Elvis said, "I'm going to have to hit the mountain. I'm sure not going to make some daddy with a carload of kids go off the side just to dodge us.

"Now, if we hit the side of the mountain it may stop us hard. Or, it could bounce us back across the road and down the side of the mountain."

Sal grabbed a piece of rope and lashed himself to a part of the interior framework. He knew we were going to roll down the side of the mountain.

Richard Davis yelled, "Where'd you get the rope?"

Sal looked at him wide eyed and shrugged.

We swooped off the shoulder of the mountain into the edge of San Bernardino. There was a traffic light about 300 yards ahead of us about to turn red. Cross traffic was about to move into our path, like grass in front of a mowing machine. There was a filling station on the right side of the road with a gravel entrance. It was real close.

"Can we get off the road here, Joe?" Elvis yelled.

"No," Joe yelled. "You're going too fast."

"We have to try it," Elvis said.

Chief, behind us in my Ford, saw we were having problems. He started weaving back and forth across the road so no one could pass.

Elvis swung off the road onto level ground in front of the gas station. He spun the wheel and went into a long skid across the loose gravel. Finally, the brakes began to grab and the whole thing sort of rocked back and settled down and sat still.

It was silent in the dark.

The engine had stalled. You could hear the guys breathing. Sal Orfice, Elvis' personal barber, gave out a long sigh. He never had been very talkative.

71

Elvis slowly opened the door. We all got out. Slowly. And walked off into the dark. Each of us went in a different direction.

Chief was just driving up when I walked around to the back of the machine and leaned against it.

Richard lay down on the ground and kissed it. He wasn't joking.

I felt sick.

Long cross-country drives were tough on the mobile home. Elvis burned out one engine after another. They just weren't built for all the long hauls we made.

Elvis decided to buy something bigger, a double decker bus. George Barris in North Hollywood customized it to suit Elvis. He put in a big bedroom for Elvis on the top deck. It was back in the rear. Next to it, he built a big kitchen. Then he put in a bathroom and a large closet for Elvis' clothes.

He put in another closet for the guys to use.

Downstairs, the bus was like a huge living room with stereo tape and radio.

The Old Green Cadillac . . .

Elvis was always intrigued with unusual pieces of machinery. Like the old 1935 Cadillac painted bright, bright green.

Eddie Fadal said one day a man showed up at the front gate at Graceland, driving it and asking for Elvis.

Elvis met Eddie, an announcer on KRLD radio in Dallas, when Elvis came through on tour in 1956. Elvis performed in the Cotton Bowl behind high chicken wire put up for protection from 26,000 screaming fans. When Elvis later went to Fort Hood for basic training, Eddie built an extra wing on his house in Waco for Elvis to use. Eddie even put in a piano for Elvis to play on.

And Elvis liked to go up in the movie projector room at Eddie's Old Texas Theater in Waco and talk to the guy about how his movie machinery worked.

Elvis looked up to Eddie as a kind of father figure because he was the oldest guy in the bunch.

Eddie tells about the old green Cadillac like this:

Elvis was sitting with us at the breakfast table at Graceland one morning. Uncle Travis called Elvis from down at the gate. He said a guy was down there with an old restored Cadillac, really beautiful, that Elvis might like to see.

Elvis said, "Sure, Uncle Travis. Send him on up here. We'll be through in a minute."

Elvis put down the phone and went on eating his breakfast. When we all got finished, Elvis went out front to take a look.

The old car was beautiful. Lots of wood molding. The paint sparkled.

You could just see Elvis falling in love with it. He was eating his heart out to buy it.

"How much do you want for it?" he said, head still under the car and sounding muffled.

The guy was absolutely confident he had a big sale. "It'll cost you $35,000 to get this one," he said.

It was a big rip-off.

Elvis looked out from under the fender, straight into my eyes. He waited.

I slowly shook my head.

Without another moment's hesitation, Elvis pulled himself up and dusted himself off. "Don't think I'm interested," he said.

The poor guy hesitated. He stuttered a couple of things. Elvis just shook his head.

The guy looked like he might cry right here. Then he got in the old green Cadillac and drove it back down the hill.

The commercial airlines wanted to make Elvis feel at ease when he finally decided he had to take planes to make all the long tours around the country.

Airport guards would open a side gate so he could drive right up to the side of the plane in his own limousine and go straight on board.

Elvis' party was seated first. Regular passengers came on next. It was funny. People coming down the aisle would spot Elvis. They would try to stop. People coming behind them would shove them on.

Stewardesses did everything to keep Elvis relaxed in the air.

One night, he took one of them by the elbow and said. "Would you tell me something, miss? Why do you always put me on the back seat of the plane? I always ride in the back seat."

She touched his cheek with the tips of her fingers.

"Why, that's so you don't have to trouble yourself to turn around when you want to talk to someone. They have to do the turning."

"Can You Keep a Secret?"

All the guys were fooled by what I was doing in the early spring of 1967. They thought I was driving Colonel Parker from his Hollywood office down to his home in Palm Springs for the weekends.

In fact, Elvis had me driving the Colonel secretly to Las Vegas.

"Charlie, can you keep a secret?" Elvis asked me one day.

"Something big?" I said.

"Priscilla and I are going to be married on the first day of May. In Las Vegas. At the Alladin Hotel. The Colonel wants it to be a nice wedding. Not a circus. He doesn't want the media to get onto it until he is ready for them."

I nodded. "That's big."

Elvis smiled. "You won't be taking the Colonel down to his place in Palm Springs, the next few weekends. You'll be driving him over to Las Vegas to the Alladin so he can get things set up."

We were out cruising the streets of Beverly Hills and swinging north along the ocean.

Elvis said it was time for him to get married. The Colonel had agreed. Priscilla had been staying at Graceland nearly five years, finishing her education at Immaculate Conception High School. She was a grown woman now. She was 21 years old. The Colonel thought it might look bad if anyone thought that she and Elvis were living together.

"You know how much I love Priscilla," he said. "I didn't want to get married this soon. But I guess the Colonel is right."

He looked out at the ocean.

"Look, Charlie, nobody knows about this but you, Marty Lacker and Joe. Keep yourself available to the Colonel. Drive him down to Las Vegas whenever he needs to get down there.

"And one other thing: don't tell anybody."

Elvis reminded me of Jimmy Wakely in a lot of ways. Both were stars who led unusual lives. But both of them, way down inside of them, were good old country boys who were always worried about doing what was the right thing.

For all of that spring, I drove the Colonel down to Las Vegas on the weekends.

As we drove, we often talked about the wedding.

The Colonel was having a ball with it.

"Now, Charlie," he said waving his big cigar, "when you finally decide to get married, let me handle it." He shot an amused glance at me. "When are you going to get married?"

"Not yet, Colonel," I said. "I'm still practicing."

He laughed.

"When you do decide, let me know," he said. "Charlie, we could make some money on it."

"Make money?" I said. "On my own wedding?"

He nodded. "Yes, we can. Now, you listen to the old Colonel."

He outlined his plan as we sped along. All typical Parker.

"I'll rent a football stadium and you and your bride will ride in to the altar, located on the 50 yard line, on a pair of big elephants." He smiled and pulled out a fresh cigar. "We'll charge admission for it."

I laughed. "Colonel, that's wild."

He waved the cigar at me like a magic wand. "It's not wild. There's money in it.

"Now you listen to the old Colonel."

It was the best kept wedding secret ever...
Elvis stands with Priscilla and Vernon
I kneel with Joe Esposito.

He'd take me into the casinos with him when he wanted to gamble. I couldn't spend a dime of my own money. He knew I loved to gamble, almost as much as he did.

He'd sit down at a roulette wheel and start putting out chips for both of us.

"Let's put a $25 chip on this square for you, Charlie," he'd say. "And some here and here and here."

Whenever I won, it would be $200.

The Colonel would say, "Now, you'd better go wire Mrs. Parker some flowers."

He winked. "Listen to the Colonel. Go wire Mrs. Parker some flowers when you win."

With the Colonel handling the whole thing like a grand master of illusions, the wedding took place quietly and was followed by a lovely breakfast on the morning of May 1, 1967, many hours before the media was able to figure out what was really going on. There were strolling violin players and flowers and happiness in heaps.

Elvis was still anxious.

He came downstairs at Graceland, not too many days later, with a worried look. He wandered into the kitchen where I sat talking to Mary Jenkins, one of Elvis' cooks.

He sat down opposite me at the table.

"I've been upstairs talking on the phone to the Colonel in Palm Springs," he said, with no further explanation.

"Well, I know it can't be too bad," I said. "He told me one day that none of us would have to start worrying so long as you could walk out on stage with no introduction and the audience goes wild."

Elvis never was introduced when he came out on stage to open a concert.

"Mary, scramble me some eggs," Elvis said.

"You want some bacon, too?" Mary said, flipping on a burner. "A little toast."

Elvis nodded.

"What's wrong?" I said.

"Aw, it's the Colonel again," he said.

"What did he say."

"Well, before I got married, the Colonel said I'd lose half of my fans if they thought we were living here at Graceland together without being married. Now, he says that I'll probably lose half of them because we did get married.

"He's a hard old man to please."

"Aw, you know how the Colonel is," I said. "He was just kidding you."

Elvis shook his head. "I don't think it's very funny. He even said that Priscilla will hurt me at the box office."

"Elvis, I was down in Las vegas with the Colonel all spring. I know how he felt about that wedding. He's just kidding you now, for some reason."

Elvis shook his head. "I don't think so, Charlie."

Sometimes you get a funny feeling about something—like a premonition or a warning of something about to happen and there is nothing you can do to stop it.

One of our Hawaiian friends once told me that when you feel something like a feather stroking the back of your neck, it's the spirit world trying to tell you something. That's the feeling I felt on the back of my neck at that moment, looking across the table at Elvis.

The Lost Diamond . . .

The same feeling came back again on the day Priscilla lost her diamond ring in the tall grass at the Circle G ranch.

It was not many days after they were married.

One reason the loss of the diamond ring hurt so much was because Priscilla didn't seem to realize she was a millionaire's wife. She was the daughter of a military man, known affectionately as an "Army brat."

79

Wedding congratulations from George Klein . . .

Mike McGregor remembers it well. He had a leather shop out behind the barn at Graceland. He made some of the big jeweled belts Elvis introduced in Las Vegas. And he did some leather clothes for Elvis—especially vests in different colors.

Elvis was proud of the people who worked around Graceland. One night he strolled out on stage in Las Vegas and opened his show by showing off a pale blue leather vest Mike had made for him.

"Mike McGregor, an old boy who works for me back in Memphis, made this for me," Elvis said, proudly.

Mike took care of everybody's horse down at the ranch—about 26 of them—and up in the barn behind Graceland.

Here's what he says about Priscilla's lost diamond:

I took care of everybody's horse. But the horses I took the best care of were Elvis' horse, Rising Sun, and Priscilla's Domino.

Elvis liked to race them. They'd go streaking up and down the hills. They'd go clattering over the wood bridge across the lake. They'd race all the way to the far side of the ranch and back.

Naturally, I tried to keep the boss' horse in better shape than the others so he could win. The boss loved winning and I wanted him to feel good about his life.

But Priscilla would try to beat him every time they raced.

Sometimes she would come out to the barn alone, and her pregnant with Lisa Marie. She'd grab a hold of Domino's mane and pull herself up on his bare back. She'd ride off across the ranch like some kind of Indian.

One time, Elvis set up a big race. Priscilla took off her diamond ring and slipped it over the end of a bandanna handkerchief. She tied it around her neck.

They all charged off. When they came thundering up to the fence on the other side of the ranch, Priscilla suddenly grabbed her throat. She looked shocked.

Elvis reined Rising Sun and wheeled him alongside Domino. "What's wrong?" he said.

"The ring," Priscilla said, feeling her bare neck. "My bandanna came off. The ring is gone."

*Elvis raised one hand like a cavalry officer and said,
"We've lost Priscilla's diamond. Go back slow and look for
it."*

*We walked the horses back slowly through the tall dry
grass, trailing Elvis and Priscilla.*

*Billy Smith got off his horse and walked ahead of it so he
could see down in the grass better.*

*I jumped off. Then everybody got down and walked. At
the top of the ridge, Priscilla stopped. Off to the right you
could see the tall white cross on the other side of the lake, the
thing that first attracted Elvis to the ranch.*

"I think this is where it may be," Priscilla said.

*She slid out of her saddle and we all got down on our
hands and knees and started poking through the grass.*

*Before long, Elvis just sat down in the dry grass. He
clasped his hands across his knees and looked off into the
distance at the soaring white cross that dominated the
skyline.*

He patted Priscilla on the back as she crawled past him.

*"Quit worrying about it, Priscilla," he said. "It was just a
diamond. We can always find another one."*

*Priscilla and the rest of us kept looking until it was nearly
dark.*

*Elvis got up and climbed into the saddle and hauled in the
reins. "Let's go gang. It's not worth it."*

Priscilla was the last to give up the search.

*Then she got on Domino and trailed us back to the
stables.*

*She came out to the barn a few days later, all by herself.
She wanted to ride Domino.*

"Can you bring her out, Mike?" she said.

*I unlatched the stall gate and reached up to get Domino's
saddle off the wall peg.*

*Priscilla put that little hand of hers on my arm. "No
saddle, Mike," she said.*

*She saw that worried look in my face. "Don't worry,
Mike. I'll be careful."*

*She walked past me into Domino's stall, got hold of its
mane and pulled herself up. She kicked its sides and Domino
trotted out of the stall and hit the outdoors flying.*

*Halfway up the ridge where she lost the diamond,
Domino swerved. Priscilla's knees couldn't hold her on its
back and she went flying through the air over Domino's
shoulder.*

When I ran up to where she was sitting in a mud puddle, a streak on her cheek, Priscilla was laughing. Domino turned and looked at her, then walked back with a whinny.

Priscilla got up and headed back toward the cottage with the bottom of her riding pants heavy with mud.

As I watched her go, it struck me that Priscilla was having some bad luck.

She never did go back up on that "lost diamond" ridge, as far as any of us know.

That lost diamond ring is still up there somewhere.

The Colonel Entertains . . .

There was always a nice feeling of "Home" with Priscilla in the house.

It was a happy time for all of us when we lived over at 1174 North Hillcrest Road.

The house overlooked Los Angeles and Beverly Hills. On a clear day, you could see planes taking off or coming in to land at International Airport.

When you said "the family" you meant Elvis and Priscilla with Lisa Marie, Elvis' cousin Patsy Gambill and her husband, Gee Gee, who was Elvis' valet and took care of all his clothes. And me.

Joe and Joanie had their own place. They came by the house a lot. So did the Colonel and his aide, Tom Diskin.

The dining room table was one of the Colonel's favorite places. He loved to sit there and puff on a big cigar and tell Elvis stories about his past exploits.

He told us about the time when he was nothing but a dog catcher in Florida. That state probably never had a dog catcher like Colonel Parker before—or after.

"I made a special box and put it on the counter in my dog catcher office," he began one night after dinner.

"It stood out like a sore thumb when you came in. You couldn't miss it."

Elvis smiled, seeing that another of the Colonel's stories was on the way.

"This box had a heavy chain around it that was locked together by a thick padlock," he said, looking around the table at everybody.

He flicked cigar ash into a tray the maid brought him after dinner.

"I lettered a little sign and put on it. The sign asked visitors to drop whatever loose change they had in their pockets through the slot in the top of the box. The proceeds would help the dog catcher do his job."

He made a hearty little chuckle and sent a cloud of blue cigar smoke puffing over the table. It smelled expensive.

"I'd close up the office around noon to go to lunch and then I'd pick up the box," he went on. "It was a special built box—with no bottom in it. All the coins that visitors had dropped through the slot were still lying there on the top of the counter, just waiting to be scooped up.

"Those coins helped buy the county dog catcher a good lunch and, on a good day, a couple of good cigars."

And the Colonel could laugh so hard that the tears would roll down his cheeks.

One of the Colonel's favorite stories was about what he called the "disappearing hot dog."

He said some of the people with the carnivals he worked with would pull the hot dog trick on customers. In preparation for the trick, they would drop a hot dog in the dust in front off the counter where customers stood to order a hot dog.

"The carney would wipe a little mustard and catsup on an empty bun and hand it to the customer. The customer would open it up and say, 'Hey, you didn't put the hot dog in it.'

"The carney would look puzzled and then lean out over the counter and look down. He'd say, 'There it is. You must have dropped it.' "

There was another carney trick the Colonel liked to tell Elvis about.

"It was a special ring," he said. "What made it special was that there was a real quarter welded to it. When you wear the ring, the welded quarter is on the palm side of your hand.

"Now, the show is on and the carney is making change on tickets. He counts out the right change in the palm of his open hand. The customer can see it. He knows it's the right change. No one is short changing him.

"Then the carney dumps the change in the customer's hand and urges him to move right along. The customer doesn't realize that a quarter of his change stayed back in the carney's palm, welded to that ring he was wearing.

"The carney could make an extra quarter on every ticket."

Priscilla didn't mind if Elvis told the guys to come by to eat with us. However, she made one restriction after a while.

You could see it coming.

"You fellows are welcome to come and eat with us," she told them one night after things in the kitchen started to get real disorganized, crowded up and milling around and yelling. It was a scene.

"But don't anyone come back in the kitchen and place some order with our maid or cook," Priscilla said.

"This is a home. It's not a short order restaurant."

The guys got the message.

Priscilla was tough. Cool. She could face you down if ever push came to shove.

Some Unusual People

Elvis liked unusual people.

Georgy Stoll was talented and eccentric.

Elvis took a liking to him.

Georgy directed the musical scores in some of Elvis' movies. He was also musical director for many of Mario Lanza's movies.

Elvis admired Mario and one of Georgy's stories that Elvis liked to hear about took place in Rome. Georgy was directing an orchestra for Mario in a great room in the Vatican itself. they were making a recording there.

Mario couldn't read a note of music. Nor could Elvis. At one point in the recording session in the Vatican, Mario stopped singing and looked down at his music stand. He stopped the music.

"Georgy, would you come over here and see if this part of the music looks right to you," Mario said.

Georgy walked over and looked down at the music stand in front of Mario.

Mario had laid out a whole series of provocative pictures on it. The singer had a crazy sense of humor, Georgy said. He shuddered, thinking of what the priests would have said.

The Old Castle

Georgy lived in a real castle that looked a thousand years old. It was located in Northern California, of all places. Up on a hillside in the Big Sur area near where Priscilla's mother and father lived.

Elvis drove us all up there to visit the Beaulieus one weekend when Priscilla was pregnant with Lisa Marie. On the way back, Elvis decided to swing off the main highway and go by the castle and see Georgy.

He patted Priscilla's tummy and said, "Maybe we ought to buy a castle for our little princess."

"What if your 'little princess' turns out to be a little prince?" she asked Elvis, although both felt sure it was going to be a boy.

Stoll's wife was lovely. Her father had been associated with Howard Hughes. When he died, he left her independently wealthy.

The old castle had been brought over from England by a California banker, stone by stone. They put it back together again up in a region of California where you can drive two or three miles between homes. Lonely. But beautiful.

One of the strange things about Georgy was that he had all his clothes tailored to look wrinkled at all times. He never would tell us why he wanted the Wrinkled Look.

Georgy and his wife didn't have any children. But she had a collection of dolls that were remarkably lifelike.

In fact, the castle was full of dolls that had been bought all over the world.

They also had a pet monkey which they dressed and treated as a real little person.

Elvis' favorite room in the old castle was the big main hall which had an enormous fireplace. The fireplace was so big and deep it looked like you could walk around inside it.

In one of the downstairs rooms they had a torture rack.

"They used to tie people on it with ropes," Georgy explained. "They could stretch victims up to 12 inches before it killed them."

The idea fascinated Georgy. He was as short as I was.

"One night, we were getting ready to go to a party," he told Elvis. "I said to my wife, 'I think I'll stretch myself a few inches for the party.'"

Elvis sat down on the edge of the rack and folded his arms.

"Mr. Stoll," he said, "is this another true story?"

Georgy nodded. "I was quite serious about it. I placed myself on the rack, just about here. Like this. I was stretched about five inches before I got up. I came out almost as tall as my wife. It was a nice feeling.

"During the party, I began shrinking slowly back to my normal size. People stared at me. They didn't really believe it."

Elvis laughed, looking at Georgy and imagining him five inches taller, then slowly shrinking back to his regular size.

Later, after we got back to Hollywood, I thought about going back up there to the old castle to see if I could make myself a few inches taller.

I never got back up there.

Was Georgy's story true? Could it be true? We never knew. Georgy's wife swore to us that it was a true story.

The Mystery Went On

No one understood why it took Priscilla so long to fix up the house at 144 Monovale in Hollywood.

When Elvis bought it, she said it had to be fixed up a lot before they could move in.

She tried to turn every house Elvis bought into a real home.

The house on Monovale once belonged to the English actor, Robert Montgomery. His daughter, Elizabeth, starred as the pretty young witch in the television series, "Bewitched."

It seemed strange. Priscilla spent a year working on it.

She would be gone for long periods, meeting with workers and designers and so on.

"How about taking me along the next time you go," Elvis often said.

She would smile and shake her head.

The mystery went on for quite a while. Then she finally announced that the place was ready to look at.

She was nervous. She watched Elvis like a hawk when he stepped inside and looked around for the first time.

Elvis said nothing but began slowly moving through the house, room by room. You could tell Priscilla was edgy.

From the foyer, you stepped down a couple of steps into an elegant living room in a beautiful green motif. Elvis' piano was in the same shade of green. The room seemed to invite you to sing.

You climbed a couple of steps to enter Elvis' private office. Priscilla had put a big television set in it with a big desk and chair plus some deep couches. The office had a library shelf that you could push back into the wall and turn into a wet bar.

Another door off the foyer led out into a formal dining room. There was a master chair for Elvis. There was a special chair for Priscilla who always sat at his left hand.

A stairway curved up to the balcony. My bedroom was at the top of the stair case. Elvis' and Priscilla's bedroom with a big fireplace was down to the right. Elvis' bath had huge closets and a barber chair. Hers had a marble bath tub, big closets and a wall mirror and bar for her ballet exercises.

Turning right, when you left my bedroom, took you to Lisa Marie's room with a window that overlooked the driveway and a greenhouse. The street was beyond.

Robert Montgomery's old gymnasium upstairs had been turned into a bedroom for Sonny West, one of Elvis' personal bodyguards, and his wife, Judy.

There was a country kitchen. Brick walls. A brick chopping block sitting in the middle.

The maid's quarters were off the kitchen.

The large grounds surrounding the house were the private domain of Priscilla's beautiful pair of Great Danes, Brutus, and his female companion, Snoopy. Brutus could easily intimidate you when he jumped up and leaned his front paws down on your shoulders.

Snoopy, on the other hand, was sweet.

When Elvis completed the tour, he turned to Priscilla. He smiled. "I like it."

She grabbed him and hugged him. They held onto each other for a long time.

One night, J.D. Sumner and the guys in his Stamps Quartet came by the place. Elvis showed them around. They ambled around the grounds.

J.D. said something about all the wealth that had descended on Elvis in California. The big homes. The expensive cars lining the driveways outside.

"Elvis," he said, "do you ever think you'll wake up one morning and find that this is all just a dream?"

Elvis nodded. "Yes, I do." He frowned a little.

"And when that question comes to him," I said, "Elvis goes in the bathroom and shuts the door. Then he jumps up and down and claps his hand and laughs like some little kid. And he says, 'It's NOT a dream!'"

J.D. started laughing like a bass drum.

We strolled around the yard a little more and talked. Then J.D. said they had better get a cab and head back to the hotel.

"Just pile in the Stutz and I'll run you back myself," I said.

"Hold it," Elvis said. "The Stutz is my own private machine."

"Okay, fella," I said, with mock hostility, playing the court jester, "if it's your little car, then you can park it yourself, next time."

Elvis was a great audience. My reply was so unexpected that he nearly fell out laughing. So I took the scene one step farther.

"Don't get smart," I said. "We're not out in the public now. And I just might knock the tar out of you if you mess with me." I walked up to him close, like a daring little rooster.

"Why you . . . " Elvis broke up laughing again at the little character I had created in front of him.

Then I switched characters into that of a lazy moving servant.

"I'se sorry, Mr. Elvis," I said with a slow lip. "I sho won't take yo cah, if'n you say I better not do it. No, suh, Mr. Elvis. I nevah would do dat."

They all got to laughing so hard that Brutus and Snoopy came running up to see what was going on.

The Land of Phantasy

People used to ask Elvis if he didn't have a ball on some of those film locations. Like being in Mexico when he made Fun in Acapulco.

"Man, we never even left the back lot at the studio for that one," he said.

"They took some long shots of someone water skiing and then some close ups of me in a studio with someone splashing water on me. It came out looking like I was out there on the water. I never got out of Hollywood. It's some of that 'film magic' they talk about."

We were out of Hollywood a lot, however, making movies.

Elvis loved it down around Sedona, Arizona where we lived while he was making Stay Away Joe.

Sedona is a beautiful little village with lots of millionaires living there. The Colonel rented Elvis a nice place there.

It was a fantasy scene at night. The moon would come up over the mesa through the trees. It would shine on a little stream that snaked through the surrounding hills.

The village was so quiet. So quiet that you listened for owls and things.

Somewhere back in the desert down there—maybe talking to one of his old retired pals from circus days in Florida—the Colonel found four little matched black ponies. Cute as they could be.

The Colonel bought them and called Mike back at Graceland to hitch up a truck to a horse trailer and come out to Arizona and pick them up.

"They have matched harnesses," the Colonel said. "They pull a little black buckboard wagon big enough for Elvis to ride on. Elvis wants to ride the buckboard and drive the ponies in parades."

I had an idea the parade thing was the Colonel's idea—not Elvis'.

We moved down to a place called Apache Junction in Arizona when Elvis signed to do Charro. It was in the foothills of the Superstition Mountains. You could see them, low in the distance. Somewhere up there was the fabled Lost Dutchman gold mine.

Elvis grew a beard for the movie. He was playing the part of a tough cowboy and pretty good gunslinger.

I started growing a beard in sympathy. So Elvis wouldn't feel bad about walking around unshaven. So did Jerry Schilling and Joe Esposito.

Gee Gee didn't grow one. He's part Indian and Indians can't grow beards.

Getting away into the desert to make a movie was great for all of us. It was a retreat from everything that caused pressure on the family.

We sat around at night, thinking about important things like lost goldmines—and wondering if we might ever be able to find it.

There was talk about beginning a search for it at the end of shooting the movie.

Elvis just smiled. "I already found it."

He began to grow curious about some of the changes being made in the script during the shooting of Charro.

"What's wrong?" I asked him.

They were setting up sun reflectors for one of the outdoor scenes with Elvis.

Elvis scratched his beard which was beginning to itch him. The director was across the road, talking to his camera man.

"Mr. Warren's been taking out all the good stuff," Elvis said. "I can't figure out why."

"What good stuff?" I said.

I started scratching my own beard. It made mine itch when I watched Elvis scratch his.

"The fights," he said. "The gunplay. All the rough stuff."

He looked up at the blue sky and the shadowy lines of the distant Superstition Mountains and the Lost Dutchman.

He hooked a thumb in his belt. "You know, Charlie," he said, "I'm beginning to feel like this Charro character. I can do him. If they'll quit messing up the script.

"I'm going to have a talk with Mr. Warren about it when we break for lunch tomorrow."

The next day, the caterers came in and set up the tables and chairs and put out lunch for everyone.

Elvis sat with the director, Charles Marcus Warren. He didn't say anything to him about the script problem during the meal.

Elvis never liked to talk too seriously during a meal if it might lead to an argument.

One night, in Hollywood, Elvis and I got into a little spat at supper. He got up and walked out. When he came back to finish eating, he said, "Charlie, let's don't ever argue like that again when we're eating. I just went back there and lost what I ate."

After lunch, Elvis said, "Mr. Warren, what are they doing to our script?"

Mr. Warren looked at his canvas shoes for a moment. Then he looked straight at Elvis.

"The studio has changed its mind about what they want you to do in this movie," he said. "They first called me and told me they wanted a good Western script for you. I came up with a story line. They liked it.

"Then, a few days ago, they called me in. They said the public is complaining about violence in movies, in books, on radio and television. They said for us to ease up on the violence in Charro."

"Ease up?" Elvis said.

"You know," Mr. Warren said. "They want us to turn all

the gunfights into dirty looks. That kind of thing."

He sighed. A troubled look came over his face for the first time since I had known this director.

"It's going to be hard to get anything going for you as an actor, Elvis," he said. "But we'll try."

Elvis nodded. "They must want a milktoast Western."

He stood up. "I'll tell you what, Mr. Warren. If that's all they want, let's just do the best we can and take the money and run."

One of the first scenes they shot at the studio after they came back in town with the location film in the can was one of Elvis riding into town as the gunfighter, Charro. Everybody is afraid of him because he has such a reputation as a fast gun.

In the scene, Elvis gets off his horse in front of the saloon and holds both hands up so that everyone can see he is unarmed, coming in peace, his hands empty. Then he walks into the saloon.

The director let me play a bit part in the scene. I play the part of a Mexican peasant standing in the street in front of the saloon. It was not a speaking part. I wore a serape over my shoulder and a big straw hat. I stood in the middle of the dusty street when Elvis came riding in.

The camera showed a closeup of me and another Mexican sighing with relief to know that Charro was not going to shoot up the place. Then they softened the edges of the barroom scenes.

That's how they changed the mood of Charro.

Elvis was concerned about the way it turned out.

"Don't worry, Elvis," I said. "It's a good movie."

People could hardly believe what went on among the guys while Elvis was making a movie—with Elvis in the middle of all of it.

When Elvis got a little bored with making Clambake, in which he plays Cowboys and Indians with a bunch of school children—using his forefinger as a make-believe gun—everybody started playing games to keep him happy on the job.

Everybody came in for our practical jokes, from the director on down to the coffee man. But they all loved it. Movie crews loved to work with Elvis and they asked to. Everyday was different from the last one and you never knew what to expect when you got up in the morning. With Elvis, life was great.

I walked out on the set of Clambake one morning. It was the original Phantom of the Opera movie set. A bucket of water hit me from way up on one of the high catwalks.

I looked up—and another bucket hit me. My shirt was soaked. I took it off and neatly placed it in front of a heater to dry out. Then I went to the wardrobe department and got a dry shirt to put on.

Every 20 minutes or so, I'd go back and feel my shirt to see if it was getting dry. It felt as wet as ever..

I couldn't understand it. At the end of the day, I checked it again. Still soaking wet! I walked away from it—then sneaked back and peered around the corner. There was Elvis—spraying it with a fire extinguisher. He had been doing that all day long. As soon as I felt it, he'd come back and spray it again.

Then Elvis came out of his dressing room to do a scene, Richard Davis, his valet, hit him from the same catwalk with a balloon filled with water.

Elvis looked up and said quietly, without anger, "I'll get you for that."

Elvis went back into his dressing room and came back out a few minutes later in a dry costume and did his scene.

Then he found a heavy fire hose—and blasted Richard off the catwalk.

The movie's director, Arthur Nadel, had been hit by firecrackers so much that he started coming to the set wearing an old Nazi war helmet.

In one scene, Elvis goes to answer a phone. The cameras are rolling. As he picks up the phone, he says, "Hello." Just then, Nadel lit a huge round firecracker and rolled it across the set floor at him.

Elvis picked up the phone, said, "Hello," then saw the lit firecracker bomb rolling toward him. He dropped the phone and yelled, "Oh, hell!" and fled.

In another scene, Bill Bixby was acting in front of the camera and Elvis simply walked up to him with a cream pie and pushed it in his face.

Pies started flying everywhere.

At the end of shooting The Trouble with Girls, a lot of Elvis' practical joke victims decided to get even with him. They all loved him, by the way. They made up a signal for the attack: When Nadel announced that the last foot of film had been shot by saying, "That's a wrap," they would all grab up hidden pies and rush Elvis.

On the last day of the shooting, Elvis realized that the movie was over but, for some strange reason, Nadel was killing time before saying, "That's a wrap."

Elvis called Richard and said, "Go find out what's going on."

That was a mistake. Richard was one of the conspirators. So Elvis never was warned.

When Nadel finally did yell, "That's a wrap," there was a screaming pie attack on Elvis and anyone else unlucky enough to be near him.

Then the attackers fled in laughter.

They ran to a little bar next door. They thought they would escape Elvis that way.

Richard tells what happened:

When we attacked Elvis, the pies flew so thick through the air that the floor of the studio got too slippery to stand on. Jerry Schilling went down. He had to be taken to the hospital.

Bill Reynolds and I thought we had escaped. He was Debbie Reynolds' brother and did makeup for Elvis. Bill had a deadly fear of snakes and we used to wind up rubber bands and put them in envelopes and toss them in his room. It made a hissing sound, like a snake, and Joe Esposito even bought a garden snake from a pet shop to toss in with the envelope.

Bill nearly died.

Well, at the bar next door to the studio, Bill was laughing and saying, "We finally got Elvis. And we got Elvis good."

Bill was feeling great—and we both knew we were safely hidden away.

I strolled out the back door for something and three guys grabbed me—one of them was Elvis.

"Richard," Elvis said, "you go back in there and tell them everything is fine. The coast is clear. You didn't see a soul out here. And we'll not give you the treatment."

I agreed.

I went back in. "The coast is clear," I told Bill.

He laughed.

Just about that time, Elvis and his gang came in all three entrances to the bar—blasting everybody with pies and whipped cream guns. They got Bill up in a corner and creamed him all over.

They destroyed that whole bar. And the customers were howling with laughter.

Nadel was very suspicious when we all gave him a big birthday party after the movie was finished. He came to the party in a tuxedo, though, and his wife in a gorgeous gown.

Nadel sat at the end of the table. We had a big cake—it must have cost us $50. We all sang Happy Birthday to him. He looked suspicious but then he started to relax. Jerry and I were singing when we picked up the cake between us and walked down to his end of the table with it.

At the end of the song, I looked at Jerry and said, "Now."

We dumped the huge cake right in his lap. His wife laughed. He looked down in his lap and started grinning. Then he jumped up and started slinging cake at everybody.

He looked as happy as a child.

It was hard for anyone to escape us, once we had an idea to pull a joke on them. We decided to throw a firecracker at a guy at a party. He discovered it and fled out the back door into the dark. He jumped into his car and sped off.

He didn't know we had dropped a firecracker in the front seat—until he turned the corner and we could see the flash of light and the guy just raise up in his seat and smoke puff out the windows.

One night, back at Graceland, a representative of the studio called. He said that Elvis would have to wear a beard like an Arab in the movie, Harem Scarum, that Elvis had signed to do. Elvis played the part of a kind of Rudolph Valentino lover.

The studio man said Elvis could grow his own beard or the studio makeup man could put a false one on him.

Elvis said, "I'll grow my own."

So Elvis stayed upstairs for the next three weeks, growing his beard. No one could get to see him. His meals were set at his door. He took them in, ate and put the tray back outside.

One day, we heard footsteps coming down the stairs. We knew it had to be Elvis.

We all stopped what we were doing and looked at the staircase.

Elvis appeared—his hair and beard solid white! He looked like Moses coming down from the mountain.

We all got down on our hands and knees.

"Hail, Moses! Hail, Moses!"

Elvis stopped before he ever got to the bottom step.

He looked at us and said, "Aw, crap." And he turned around and went back upstairs.

A Man Of Mystery . . .

Elvis liked being known as a man of mystery. I came in one night after working for six weeks at Lake Tahoe and Reno with Jimmy Wakely. It was around four in the morning.

My phone rang. It was Joe, calling from his home in Los Angeles.

"Tomorrow, when you wake up," he said, "don't run off anywhere. Elvis has plans for you."

"For me?" I said. "Like what?"

"Tomorrow, Charlie," he said, and hung up.

Elvis liked secrets. Only he couldn't keep them.

He would tell you something and then add quietly, "Be sure you don't tell anybody about this."

He wanted to be the one who told it around.

Priscilla was always saying that Elvis could never keep a secret.

"If you want everybody to know something," she said, "just tell Elvis and tell him it is a secret."

Joe drove over the next morning to see me. Elvis was still asleep upstairs.

"What's the big deal, Joe?" I said.

"Elvis is going out to Hawaii to make Paradise, Hawaiian Style," he said. "He wants to know how long you're going to be home off the road."

"Six or eight weeks," I said.

He pulled an envelope out of his coat pocket.

"Here's your ticket," he said. "Elvis wants you to go.'"

I glanced at the name on the envelope he handed me.

I handed it back.

"This is for one Lamar Fike," I said.

He shook his head and shoved it back across the coffee table.

"Joe, do I really look like Lamar to you?" I said.

Joe laughed. He was being patient.

"Elvis has started flying, lately," he explained. "He's been using your name to buy his airplane tickets. That way, not everybody knows ahead of time that it's Elvis travelling. He's been going out as 'Charlie Hodge.' Nobody's going to bother him with a name like that."

We both laughed.

"So, he's flying out to Hawaii as 'Charlie Hodge' and I have to go as 'Lamar Fike.' Right?" I said.

He smiled. "You got it."

I picked up my ticket.

"Well, if Lamar won't say anything, then I won't either," I said.

Hawaii was one of Elvis' favorite places to vacation. We went out there many times during the years.

He loved going back and back to the Coconut Palms Hotel because he stayed there while he was making Blue Hawaii.

Behind the hotel was a row of royal Hawaiian huts. Over

the beds were crossed ceremonial spears. Each of the huts had its own indoor bath along with an outdoor bath carved out of lava stone. They were shielded from prying eyes by high bamboo fences.

Sometimes they caught girls trying to climb the fence behind Elvis' hut.

Still, the huts gave you a feeling of being native. Royal native.

"We'll take the whole row of 'em," Elvis said. "It will take that many to put us all up."

Joe and Joanie took the first hut. Elvis and Priscilla took the second. Lisa Marie and her nurse took the third one. Then came Patsy and Gee Gee. I moved into the last hut in the row.

You can see Elvis' hut in the background of some of the Blue Hawaii scenes, especially the wedding barge scene.

The hotel's restaurant and lounge were on opposite sides of the entrance. Both opened onto a little stream running past the hotel. You could sit inside and pitch bread crumbs and cracker bits to the fish.

You had to walk across a little bridge to get to the huts.

Elvis loved all the Hawaiian ceremonies and pageantry at dinner time. To announce dinner, the hotel set signal fires among the trees.

They cooked pigs and fruits and vegetables wrapped in palm leaves in outdoor pits heated with hot coals.

"All this place needs is the Peabody ducks," Elvis said.

The ducks were known around the world for playing in the fountain of the Hotel Peabody lobby in downtown Memphis.

Elvis loved to sit around and talk and watch all the action.

One night, during dinner, he started to tell us about Norman Taurog, one of his favorite directors. Mr. Taurog spoke with a distinctive accent. He came out to Hawaii to direct Elvis in Blue Hawaii.

"Mr. Taurog said I always reminded him of his own early days out in Hollywood," Elvis said, lighting up a long thin cigar, the kind he loved to puff when he wasn't recording or singing on the road.

"He was directing motion pictures while he was still in his teens, if you can believe it.

"Elvis, we both were wealthy teen-agers," he used to say.

"He had a ton of money when he was a kid. A lot of big cars. A lot of dressy clothes.

"He said girls followed him around in packs. Everywhere he went. They were hanging on him. He had guys around, just like me. His personal 'entourage,' he called them.

"I told him, 'They call mine the 'Memphis Mafia.' He got a kick out of that."

The nice smells of Hawaiian cooking drifted through the air from the open pits.

Elvis tapped the ash off his cigar and studied the greyed fire end.

"He's got glaucoma now," he said. "Eyes so clouded over he can't even see the scenes good through the camera lens. He has to take the word of an assistant director on how it all looks to the camera."

Elvis remained loyal to Mr. Taurog, even after he couldn't do his job so well.

"How come?" I asked him once.

"He needs to feel he's still needed," Elvis said.

One day Elvis bought a limousine and had it sent over to Mr. Taurog's home.

"When one of the great men steps out," Elvis said, "he should go in his own limousine."

After we would finish dinner, the Hawaiian band would move back across the foyer and into the hotel lounge to play for dancing.

Elvis would get up from the table and walk out in the foyer and sign autographs for people who had been waiting on him out there. Then we would all go over to the lounge for a while.

Elvis enjoyed sitting and listening to the Hawaiian songs the men sang with their high voices and beautiful harmonies.

Nobody in our group would be dancing so I would get up and ask Priscilla to dance. Just to break the ice. I'd come back with her and take Patsy out on the floor. Then I'd dance with Joanie.

Finally, the guys would get up the nerve to dance.

When a slow number began, Elvis would get up and ask Priscilla to dance with him. Then, pretty soon, he'd say, "Cilla, I guess we better go see how the baby is getting along and put her to bed."

The other hotel guests sitting around in the lounge would usually hold back to see how Elvis and the guys did on the dance floor. Then they'd come out and join them, even try to start conversations with them. The Memphis Mafia couldn't scare you with their dancing.

Lisa Marie, of course, would be getting along just fine. She had her own royal hut to play around in. She had her own maid. She was treated like an island princess.

But Priscilla would nod when Elvis suggested they take a look. She would get up.

"I think you're right."

Elvis loved the Islands.

The Navy always put their Admiral's Barge at his disposal. He had given a special concert to help pay for the big Navy memorial built in Pearl Harbor. Beneath the imposing memorial lies the sunken battleship *USS Arizona*.

Whenever Elvis went out to Hawaii he liked to take his people out to visit the memorial. He was proud of his part in building it.

You could look down in the water and see the big ship lying on the bottom. The water was that clear. You could see a line of fuel oil still seeping up out of the fuel tanks after all those years.

Elvis loved the true Hawaiians.

There were only a hundred or so of them left, so we were told.

Elvis especially liked one big Hawaiian named Sam. Sam had a Cadillac limousine for hire. The limousine was big enough for all seven of us so we could ride around in the same car.

Joe would call ahead from back at Graceland to make sure Sam was waiting for us when we flew in. Joe would also contact the Honolulu police to see if any off-duty policemen would like to work as security for Elvis while he was out there.

Sam had all kinds of native wisdom. When Elvis got a slight sunburn on the beach, one day, Sam put vinegar on it.

"An old Hawaiian cure, Elvis," he said.

And it worked like an old Hawaiian charm.

Elvis always felt comfortable around Sam. I think it was because Sam threw in and helped us with whatever we were doing. When Elvis wanted hamburgers, Sam jumped in and started getting the charcoal going. Sam tried to make himself a part of the family.

Sam had a fantastic way of getting rid of hangovers.

When Elvis heard about it, he could hardly believe it.

Sam said he had picked it up while working as a deep sea diver for the Navy after the war was over.

"If I had a real bad headache," Sam explained to Elvis, "I would go down on the sea bottom and lie there and sleep a while in my deep sea gear. If the boys on the boat, up on the surface above me, saw a Navy officer coming our way, they would ring the phone in my ears. They would wake me up. I could move around so it would look like I had been doing something down there."

"That was some kind of wake up service," Elvis said.

One morning in the islands, Elvis felt like doing some deep sea fishing. He told Joe to charter one of the big boats so we could all go along.

Joe got one that was 40 feet long, a sleek white beauty.

We all got dressed up like so many tourists from the mainland except Elvis, who was in blues and a captain's hat. (That's where the book cover picture was taken.) Priscilla wore a big old floppy white hat. It was so huge it shaded Lisa Marie whom she was carrying in her arms when she came down the gangplank.

We headed out for the open sea. The horizon was clear and a brilliant sun lit a bright blue sky that only had a few white clouds floating here and there in it.

The moment we cleared the harbor, I felt those giant sea swells that must have been a mile deep.

Way out at sea, when we could no longer look back and see land, the crew set the heavy fishing poles with the baited lines trailing behind and alongside us.

Elvis handed around some seasick pills he had brought along so the trip would not be spoiled by everybody getting sick all over the boat.

One of those pills and you don't get seasick. You get sleepy. You don't start looking for a fishing pole. You look around for a soft bed. A flat place of any kind.

At least, that's what we all began to do.

Elvis and several others stretched out on deck in that warm sunshine.

I went below and found a couch just meant for a doze.

They were still stretched out on deck when I came back topside, yawning.

The fishing poles stood out straight. No sign of a single bite.

"This is my kind of fishing trip," I said.

The Gold Berretta...

Elvis was resting in his dressing room right after the "Aloha From Hawaii" television special seen by two billion people around the world.

One of the guys came in. "Elvis, there's a guy out here that wants to see you. It's Jack Lord."

Elvis tossed down the towel and looked up with a big smile. "Oh, yeah? Send him on in."

Elvis was tickled to death.

Jack lived on the island of Oahu and starred in the television series, "Hawaii Five-O." Each television segment opened with a close shot of Jack standing on a balcony of the Ilikai Hotel.

Elvis watched the show every week, back at Graceland or wherever he was. He admired Jack but had never met him.

Elvis wiped the sweat off his face and neck again. He always worked like a horse on stage. He gave his fans all he had.

Jack came in and shook Elvis' hand. They liked each other from the start.

"The show okay?" Elvis asked.

Jack smiled. "You didn't see me standing up on my chair and whistling?"

Elvis laughed. "The spotlights pretty well blind me, after I'm out there so long," he said.

"You know, a whistle can be the highest compliment," Jack said. "It's a tradition of the theater world, a high compliment between one actor and another.

"At that moment, I wanted every person in this auditorium to stand up and cheer.

"I don't mean that as flattery. It means I suddenly got a gut feeling of the kind of thing you were going through on stage.

"I have never heard such dramatic music in my life. Not anywhere. From anyone."

Elvis pointed a finger at me. "Charlie, get this man a chair. We don't want to lose him."

Lord took a chair and crossed his slender legs.

"Marie, my wife, and I want you and Priscilla to bring your entire party over to our place one night this week.

105

Please, come." He looked around the room. "Everyone. Please, come. We want you to."

Lord's condominium faced the ocean on the Oahu side of the island. It was gorgeous. The walls were covered with beautiful paintings.

Jack and Marie took Elvis and everyone on a tour of their place as soon as we all arrived.

Elvis kept noticing Jack's signature in the lower corner of the paintings.

"You're also an artist, Jack?" he said.

"That was my first career ambition," Jack said. "I studied art back in New York. The acting thing just sort of happened."

"It's amazing how a thing like that can run away with you," Elvis said.

Jack nodded. "You've noticed."

The other thing Elvis kept noticing as he wandered through the place was all the guitars and other kinds of musical instruments.

In one music case by a window was a banjo. It was no ordinary banjo. I had heard stories about this one but I had never seen one. There were only about 20 of them made.

Jack took it out of the case and handed it to Elvis. It was an early 1900s Gibson. The remarkable thing was that it had six strings instead of the normal five strings. This banjo could be tuned and played like an ordinary guitar.

Elvis strummed it. It was out of tune.

"Do you play all these instruments around here?" Elvis said.

"Not well," Jack said. "I try, of course. I've loved music all my life. All kinds of music. Marie is a great lover of music, as well. We're two of your greatest fans, Elvis."

Elvis patted his shoulder affectionately and said, "Thanks, Jack. That's something special to me, coming from you guys."

Jack seemed really touched.

Elvis and Priscilla wandered off toward the punch bowl.

I bumped into Jack a few minutes later, in one of the halls. "Charlie, I want you to do something for me," he said. He found the case with the Gibson banjo and he got it out.

"I've decided to give this to Elvis," he said. He turned it in his hands, looking at it. "When you get back to Los Angeles, would you see that new strings are put on it for me?"

"Don't do it, Jack," I said.

He had started down the hall. Now he turned back.

"Why not?" he asked.

"Don't do it," I said. "I'm very serious. Oh, Elvis would appreciate it. But he just wouldn't play it very much. Maybe a little. Then he'd put it aside and forget it. I know him."

Jack shook his head. "Did you see what he handed me when he walked in tonight?" he said.

"What was that?" I said.

"He walked in with a matched pair of Berrettas," Jack said.

"For personal security," I said.

"I admired them," Jack said. "He gave them to me. So I want to give him something. I really want him to have this banjo. It's very rare, you know."

"Very rare," I said. "I know all about them. Well, I'll make you a promise. It won't get stacked away somewhere in the attic with all the other stuff he gets. Even if I have to keep it out in my room where he'll be sure to see it."

I kept my promise as long as I lived at Graceland—which was many months after Elvis died.

In Elvis' upstairs suite was his private office. In it, Elvis kept a piano, an organ and his own personal guitar.

Leaning in one corner of the office was Jack Lord's six-string banjo.

Cheap Guitars And Expensive Champagne . . .

Elvis considered Jack Lord one of his two best friends in the entertainment world.

107

The other was Tom Jones.

Tom was entertaining downstairs at the Ilikai Hotel when we flew out to the Islands for a break from making movies, one year.

We went to see his show, slipping into our seats after the lights had gone down. But they told Tom that Elvis had come in. Tom had the house lights brought up and he introduced Elvis to the house. It took him a while to get control back.

Tom invited us all up to his suite after the show.

"I'm checking out of the hotel and moving over to a house on Kailua Bay," Elvis told Tom. "I want you to come over."

We moved the next day. Joe and Joanie stayed on at the hotel a couple of more days and then they came on over.

They brought Tom with them.

Tom and Elvis swam far out in the bay and came back in, talking all the while about music and the stage.

Everybody was in and out of the sea.

At the end of the day we were as salty as canned anchovies. When Elvis got back up to the house he went out back, climbed up on a swimming pool slide and sailed down it into the fresh water to get the salt off. The rest of us formed a line on the ladder and followed him in.

That night, Elvis sent me down to the little town of Kailua.

"I saw some guitars in a little drugstore window when we came through," he said. "Pick up a couple for us."

Joe had brought along some of Tom's favorite champagne, Dom Perignon.

We whanged cheap guitars and drank expensive champagne far into the night. And we sang. Oh, how we sang.

The only thing that slowed us down was having to stop to retune those cheap guitars.

Lamar and Tom got into a drinking contest.

Lamar lost. He came out of the bathroom finally, muttering, "My God, I'm stone blind."

His wife, Nora, led him off somewhere.

It was around dawn when Joe and Joanie left to take Tom back to the Ilikai Hotel.

Elvis loved to come back to Kailua Bay.

The people of the village left him alone to enjoy himself. He could walk along the beach and nobody would jump up from behind a bush and rush at him.

Nice waves rolled in at Kailua beach. Not those big overpowering rollers that can come in at Sunset Beach. Elvis would walk out into the bay at Kailua for a hundred yards and the sea would only come up to his chest.

Joe was always carrying his movie camera. As soon as he would see Elvis coming out of the house and heading down to the beach in his little red bathing suit he would whip up his camera.

Elvis would usually hold up his hand and turn away from the camera. He didn't like pictures taken of his bare chest. So it was only rarely that you would see him walking down to the beach without a tee-shirt on. Or a beach robe.

When we stayed over on the Honolulu side, Elvis liked to put on his scuba gear and swim far out to the reef to watch the fish that lived in the deep blue.

Our house over there was the same one that Jackie Kennedy occupied when she flew over.

Getting Ready...

Everything happening to me seemed to be getting me ready to help Elvis put together a stage show when the time came.

I started putting together my Foggy River boys right after we got to California when we came home from Germany. It wasn't easy. I lived at the YMCA in Santa Anna and did anything to stay alive. I even dressed up like a bunny rabbit and pulled a cannon in the Christmas Parade at Disneyland in Anaheim in 1960. Kids could come up and pat my stomach.

That's what you call real dedication to show business.

Thanks be to Elvis, I met Lindalee Wakely at Elvis' suite at the Beverly Wilshire Hotel. She mentioned me to her father and he hired the Foggy River boys to go out on the Nevada circuit with his show.

Jimmy hired us to open with him on the same bill with Bob Wills and the Texas Playboys at the Golden Nugget in Las Vegas. Coming off the bunny rabbit act at Disneyland, that had to be one of the biggest turn arounds in show business history.

The quartet broke up but I stayed on with Jimmy's show. We left Las Vegas to play in places like Harrah's in Reno and Lake Tahoe, the Commercial Hotel in Elko and at Cactus Pete's in Jackpot.

The only thing moving in Jackpot was the tumbleweeds flying across the highway. It was strictly a gambling location on the highway. All they had were here gambling saloons.

Plus a couple of motels. People who worked in the clubs lived in house trailers. It was a long way across the desert to the nearest grocery store.

We came back in to Las Vegas to work at the Mint. Wayne Newton was working at the Freemont Hotel and Roy Clark was over at the Thunderbird Hotel and living at the Ferguson-Franklin Hotel in a room just down the hall from mine.

Jimmy was a real power in music. He came out of Oklahoma to work with Gene Autry and soon was making his own "singing cowboy" movies and running his own network radio show. I first met him when he guest starred on the Ozark Jubilee in Springfield.

Me and my Foggy River boys backed him on that guest spot.

The first time Jimmy came up to Elvis' suite in Las Vegas Elvis got up on a piano stool and said, "Listen, everybody. This man is Mr. Jimmy Wakely. I listened to him and admired him since I was a kid. I'm honored that he came by to visit. Be nice to him because I want him to come back often."

Jimmy was so touched that he almost cried. He said, "Elvis I didn't know you kids today paid that much attention to those of us on the other side of the generation gap."

Elvis jumped down and smiled and put an arm around his shoulder. He looked back at Vernon who was sitting behind him and said, "We're not bothered by any generation gap around here, are we?"

Vernon smiled and shook his head. "No, son."

Jimmy was a change of pace in those Nevada saloons. The air would be dense with alcohol fumes. The dice would be rattling and galloping across the green felt and bouncing off the backboards. Slot machines would whirr and *chink, chink, chink*.

Then Jimmy would step up to the microphone with the quartet. He'd sing bass. I was on high tenor. We'd do a beautiful old gospel song. People would stop and look up at us and they'd try to be quiet. The waitresses would set the glasses down gently.

We did the kind of close harmonies that Glenn Miller was famous for. We did Western classics like "Tumbling Tumbleweeds." We did regular hymns like "Amazing Grace." If a piece of music was good on stage, we did it. Great variety was a hallmark.

Jimmy made the first record to hit the top of all three charts, rhythm and blues, country and Western and pop. It was "Slipping Around" which he recorded with pop star Margaret Whiting.

Trumpeter Harry James came in all the time to listen to our show. His drummer, Buddy Rich, sat in with us on drums one night at Lake Tahoe. "It's a tough gig," he said, "keeping up with you guys." Ray Charles would sit in the back and sway to things we did like 'Freight Train Blues."

Jimmy did it all. He turned everybody on.

The Lady Who Could Handle Cowboys . . .

One night I came back in from Nevada. It was so late I didn't expect anybody to be up.

I had trouble getting the front door key to work. Elvis opened it and stood there looking at me.

"Where have you been?" he said.

"Out in Nevada," I said, walking around him into the living room. I slumped onto a couch. Bone tired.

Elvis snapped the top off a bottle of pop and sat down across the room. "How'd it go?" he said. He took a long swig. "You see anybody?"

I studied him a moment.

"I spent most of the time out in Elko," I said. "Elvis, you wouldn't believe some of the characters that drift in that town."

He smiled slowly. "Tell me."

"Well, you got your real working cowboys that pack out the clubs every night. They come straight in off the ranch with their work clothes still on. You see the cattle manure stuck under the boot heels. When you mix that with the smell of whiskey, you got an odor you'll never forget as long as you live."

I got some ice and started mixing a drink.

Elvis seemed to be waiting.

"There was this beautiful blonde that showed up in Elko every Saturday night. She had been a model in New York City. One of the big ranchers outside Elko had met her and married her and brought her back with him. Really beautiful, Elvis. I can't imagine why she'd want to leave New York and settle down on a ranch out West."

Elvis finished his pop and set the bottle on a table. "Maybe she was just tired of all that phony stuff she was into back in the city."

I sat back down with my drink.

"I guess that was it," I said. "But this blonde would show up every Saturday night at our club in Elko with a pickup truck loaded with cowboys."

He grinned. "They were all with her?"

"Yea, but they were cowboys off her husband's ranch. She would drive them in to the Commercial Hotel and just turn them loose, like mustangs out of a corral. They drank, messed around with women at the bordello across the railroad tracks, and gambled. It looked like they would lose their whole week's wages before they'd get up from the gambling tables."

"What would the blonde do?" Elvis said.

"Oh, she'd settle down with a glass of bubbly at Inez Wakely's table. They'd sit and talk all evening. Along about midnight the blonde would round up all her cowboys and haul them back out to the ranch."

I sank down a little further in the couch. It felt good. "Yea, for a pretty city lady, she had learned how to handle those cowboys real well," I said.

Elvis smiled. "Some time I may go with you," he said.

Ann-Margret knew all about life in Elko.

Elvis was in Hollywood, making Viva, Las Vegas with her as his co-star. In one scene, Ann-Margaret and Elvis do a dance. You can see a shadow on the wall of a musician playing a guitar. That's me. I saved the studio a lot of money, having my shadow represent a full band.

I was leaving the movie studio one day. I looked in on Elvis' dressing room. Ann-Margret was there with a script in her hand.

"Annie," I said, "I'll see you guys in a few weeks."

"Where are you going?" she said.

"Elko, Nevada," I said.

"The Commercial Hotel?" she said.

"You know the Commercial?" I said.

"Oh, sure. I was up there three years ago. Singing with a band." She grinned.

Elvis just looked up from his script.

It was between scenes. They were dating pretty heavy.

"Tell all the cowboys hello for her," Elvis said.

She winked. "Don't tell them anything else."

They went back to studying their lines.

Just down the street from the Commercial Hotel was the Ranch Inn. We played there one month. That month, the Chad Mitchell Trio was on the bill under us. They had a nice young bass player with them who grinned an awful lot. His name was Henry John Deutschendorf, Jr. He changed his name later to John Denver—a name many people found easier to remember.

Things slowly came unglued.

I was leading three lives and wondering why I felt so tired all the time.

I was doing bit parts in Elvis' movies when I was in town. I was making trips with him to Hawaii, Memphis, Las Vegas and other places. I was working the long and really tough Nevada circuit with Jimmy Wakely.

Up at Lake Tahoe one night, I was sitting in the restaurant with Jimmy. It was late. Near the end of the engagement there. Four shows a night. Three weeks there and three weeks following that at Reno.

"What's wrong, Charlie?" Jimmy said, looking at the cold sandwich on my plate. Untouched.

I kept playing Keno. It was a passion with both of us. We could sit and play Keno, hour after hour.

I didn't want to hurt Jimmy. He was like my own Dad to me. He had taught me so much about running a stage show.

But something inside me was so tired that I wanted to walk off into the night and lie down somewhere in the desert and do nothing for a while but soak up the tranquil beauty and silence.

"I'm starting to wear down, Jimmy," I said. "And me still a young man. At least, on the outside."

I watched the people around me in the club.

"Everything is so busy and disorganized now. You know, I don't really have much of a life of my own. Not much reason to any of it. Or it doesn't seem to have any."

Jimmy nodded. He looked at his watch. It was almost time for the next show.

"Charlie, you ought to go home to Alabama and see your folks a while. That's what you need when you feel like this. Take a few days off. Go home."

I shook my head.

"Naw," I said. "I'm dropping all the other stuff. I'll just work full time for Elvis awhile. I think that's the way I have to go now."

The year was 1966.

Jimmy's face went slightly wry.

"I think you've got far too much talent to turn yourself into an errand boy for anybody. Even Elvis," he said.

"I don't think I'll exactly be an errand boy, Jimmy," I said, "I'll be in music.

Inez Wakely remembers that night:

> Jimmy didn't want Charlie to leave.
> "I can't keep the show going without Charlie," he said.
> Charlie had learned how to lay out a whole show and keep it all going. If something went wrong, Charlie knew how to handle it. That means a lot to the star.
> And Charlie was a charmer. He made people laugh.

"I Feel Like I've Lost It. . ."

After keeping Elvis off the concert stage for an incredible eight years, Colonel Parker signed him to walk back on it on July 26, 1969.

Elvis had been away from working with a live audience since early in 1961. That was when he went out to Hawaii to help raise money to build the memorial to the men of the *USS Arizona*. The one exception was the studio audience for his Singer Special in 1968, a few months after Lisa Marie was born.

The Colonel's contract called for Elvis to face the toughest audience in America on his return, the Las Vegas crowd.

Las Vegas was tough. I had faced it more than once. with my own quartet and with the Jimmy Wakely Show.

Elvis had a special reason for knowing that Las Vegas was tough.

He was sitting around his place in Trousdale Estates near Beverly Hills, one night, soon after the Colonel had signed the contract.

It was after one o'clock in the morning. Everybody had gone to bed. Priscilla, Patsy and Gee Gee.

It was one of those nights when Elvis needed to talk.

"I'm 33," he began.

"I've done all those years of crumby movie songs. A lot of things I'm not happy about."

He walked over the piano and poked one of the keys. "I feel like I've lost it."

It's a real scary feeling, hearing a talent like Elvis say he knows he can't sing like he used to. He can't sing like he was meant to. Down in his soul, he's beginning to be afraid.

Whatever else might happen in Las Vegas, Elvis did not want a repeat of his first time there.

In the spring of 1956, the Colonel had sent Elvis and his rock 'n roll combo into the New Frontier. They had puzzled the crowds there for two weeks. People sat with jaded eyes and wondered what this manic hillbilly from Tennessee was trying to do up there on stage.

Elvis' fans were not part of the New Frontier crowd then. They were still too young to get in.

Their time would come.

Elvis and Las Vegas didn't understand each other in 1956. They didn't really like each other.

Elvis left town swearing, "I'll never come back."

It was worse than the first time he went up to Nashville to appear on the Grand Ole Opry. The kings of country turned thumbs down on this strange cat with sideburns that sprang out of the cotton patch.

Elvis stood at the picture window. He looked out at the darkness.

"Look, Elvis, if you want me to, I can help you get ready," I said. "Maybe it was some kind of destiny that made me leave Jimmy when I did. So I'd be around for that Singer thing—and now this. But there's one thing I can't do. I can't tell you to rehearse. It's your house, man. But any time of the day or night that you want me, I'm here to help."

He nodded. "Thanks, Charlie. Let's start. Right now."

I picked up a song, one of the big ones, and played it on the piano. It sounded reassuring.

"Let's stay mostly with the gold," I said.

Elvis smiled.

He felt better at once. "Right. This is no time to go experimental on a bunch of new material. Yea. go with the gold."

I suddenly remembered how we had loved to sing

together from the start. On the troop ship going overseas. At the Park Hotel and the house on Goethestrasse. Riding around Paris in a taxi.

I had never ridden around in a tank with Elvis but, if I had, you'd have heard two-part harmony coming out of the metal shell. We even harmonized on Elvis' first album after coming home from Germany.

Wandering around Graceland many times, he would begin singing something and I would pick up on the harmony, sometimes from another part of the house. It created a beautiful effect.

Now, I looked up at him over the piano.

"Do you remember us singing together like this in Germany?" I said.

He chuckled. "I sure do."

For some reason, it embarrassed me slightly.

"I don't know if there is anything to having past lives," I said. "But I used to wonder in Germany if we had done some singing like that in some other life. I'd look in your eyes and think I saw something special, like I had seen your eyes before. It was a little frightening sometimes. I didn't know what it was. I often wondered if you and I had been in another life together.

"Did you ever get that kind of feeling?"

He chuckled. "Yea, I did. Sometimes."

"Oh, it was never anything like a fascination with a woman," I said. "It was just like we had been somewhere else together. One of these days, I'd like to do a regression with a hypnotist. I want to find out if we actually did something in some earlier life."

He nodded. "That's fine. But right now we've got a show to do."

I found myself in the strange position of being a vocal coach for Elvis Presley.

We started out on some of the basics of singing, just to strengthen the voice. Things like lip and tongue exercises. Like trying to widen his vocal range by singing a song in a higher and higher step until you are a full octave higher than where you began.

Elvis ended up with a working range of two and a half octaves.

Wandering around the house, or out driving around Beverly Hills, Elvis would be singing little lip exercises like Ma, Me, Mi, Mo, Mu—then go up one step and repeat it. He'd do tongue exercises like La, Le, Li, Lo, Lu—then go up one step and repeat it.

Elvis would suddenly stop and laugh, sometimes in the middle of traffic.

"Do you realize, if someone heard me now they would think I had gone bananas."

A few nights later, everybody was packed off to bed, asleep.

Elvis got up from the piano stool by me and walked over and slumped down on a couch. He stared out at the night lights reflecting on the surface of the pool. Touching the sides of statues.

"I've done so many movie songs that I may have forgotten how to do a real song," he said.

A lot of times it would be five o'clock in the morning and I would still be playing the piano and Elvis would be standing by me, singing, making echoes in our minds of other times and other stages.

The fans could hear us all the way to the front gate. They knew Las Vegas was ahead and they were sweating it out with us all the way.

One morning, when it was getting light enough outside to see some trees, Elvis got up from the piano bench and stretched.

We had forgotten to eat supper.

"Charlie, even after all those 'Elvis Presley movies' I'm going to have to do an 'Elvis Presley stage show,'" he said. "That's the way they still think of me—rock 'n roll and some ballads."

Somehow, during the many nights of rehearsal of the old songs, he had come to terms with his voice of the late '60s, deeper and richer and more complex than when he was a raw hillbilly cat growling and howling his way to fame on the Louisiana Hayride. He felt a new physical power, more subtle than a gyrating pelvis. His face was capable of more expressions than a simple sneer to churn up the fears in a young girl's heart.

"Let's get a rehearsal studio from RCA and bring in some musicians," Elvis said.

"We need to start timing some songs and lay out a show," I said. "You'll only have 45 minutes."

We went over to the bar, still talking. I mixed myself a drink. Elvis pulled a soft drink out for himself. Some people would have nearly fainted if they had seen him waiting on himself.

"We have to get some heavy sound on stage with us," he said. "Who can handle lead guitar? I want to have my own band on stage behind me, along with the hotel orchestra."

"I think James Burton is the best studio guitarist on the coast," I said. "I see him sometimes out at the Palomino Club. We've sat in together out there. I'll talk to him."

He nodded.

An RCA man later suggested Burton, also.

"We'll get a studio and start running through some things and listening to talent," I said. "Then we can lay out the show. We're going to need some dramatics. Peaks and valleys."

Elvis nodded. "Lots of them."

RCA started sending down a lot of talent for us to audition at the studio. One by one, the top men came and joined us. Jerry Sheff on bass. Larry Muhoberac on piano. John Wilkerson on rhythm guitar. I would take acoustic guitar and sing with Elvis. James Burton would take lead guitar.

Elvis heard the fire in Ronnie Tutt's drums. "Man, I've got to have him behind me," he said.

With the opening date in Las Vegas rushing at us, we did two hard weeks of rehearsal with the band at the RCA studio before moving down to the Las Vegas desert for the last two weeks before opening night.

Elvis called in The Imperials quartet. He heard a recording by the Sweet Inspirations and brought them in, too.

"How are going to finish a show like this?" Elvis said one day during rehearsal.

"It would be beautiful—and different—if you ended with a ballad like 'Can't Help Falling In Love With You,'" I said. "Then into a hard rock walk-off with a vamp. That way, they'll never know you ended a concert on a ballad."

"That's different, all right," Elvis said.

"Can't Help Falling In Love With You" became his signature song, the one he ended on, and he never changed it.

I remembered Jimmy Wakely ending his show on a ballad like that, sometimes. It was beautiful and now it was a part of Elvis.

Elvis stepped up the pace of the rehearsals.

Joe had a stop watch on everything we did, timing every number.

Haunting nighttime Las Vegas was a natural for Elvis. And it was part of getting set.

"He's a real night person," Priscilla used to say.

The huge new International Hotel had just opened in town. Elvis had been offered the star spot during opening month. The Colonel said, "No, sir." The Colonel wanted somebody else to work out all the bugs in the hotel's big Showroom. Then Elvis would come in.

So the hotel brought in the sensation, Barbara Streisand from New York City, to kick off the first month. People said Barbara would kick up a sandstorm.

Elvis sneaked us all into the cavernous Showroom one night after the lights went down, to take a look at the room in operation.

Barbara, the toast of New York, was up on the big stage alone. She had a thousand sparklers on a tight fitting gown. She was radiant. The songs had international class.

Elvis nudged me.

"Charlie, she looks awful lonesome up there by herself," he said. "God, that's an awful big stage to fill." He shook his head. "Even with a band behind you, you could get lost up there. We'll always keep my personal band out in front of the orchestra. Close to me."

"Yea, and we can put all the voices over on this side of the stage," I said.

He nodded. "I'm not going to walk out on that stage and start out by feeling I'm out there by myself."

We headed back outside.

"Let's run by The Flamingo and see Tom," Elvis said.

We had seen Tom Jones working through the years. Elvis first met him when Tom came by Elvis' movie sets in Hollywood when Tom was first successful and came to the United States.

Watching Tom on stage at The Flamingo made Elvis feel better. They had been friends a long time. And Tom's show was physical, like Elvis' stage appearances had been from the very beginning.

Tom wore a tuxedo in his act. In fact, everybody out there except Harry Belafonte wore a tuxedo.

"I never felt good in a tuxedo on stage," Elvis said. "I wore one for the Sinatra show at the Fontainebleau in Miami. I never felt good in it."

We sneaked into our booth at The Flamingo so neatly that the audience didn't realize Elvis was there.

Tom was a powerhouse on stage. He was belting out stuff like a Welsh coal miner with a big shovel. In a tuxedo.

"I'd feel a lot better in a *gi* than in a tuxedo," Elvis whispered. The *gi* is the loose fitting outfit of the karate performer.

Elvis nudged me. "Priscilla has Bill Belew making me some *gis* for the opening. But don't tell anyone."

Elvis had been studying karate for years. Experts said he had the most graceful power moves they had ever known.

Now, Priscilla herself had taken it up.

Elvis had his black belt in the martial art. He loved karate next to performing on stage.

He planned to combine the two on stage.

We went backstage after Tom's show.

At Home On The Vast Stage . . .

Elvis began to feel at home on the vast stage of the Showroom at the International. He began to dominate the space that already was beginning to scare off other entertainers.

We walked into the Showroom for a late afternoon rehearsal a few days before the opening. The great gold curtain was pulled back, revealing the giant stage.

Elvis had brought an awful lot of good people together. Great people.

"Look at that stage, Charlie," he said. "There's every kind of music up there that I ever wanted to be around."

The flat lights on the stage flooded over a swarm of talent.

The Imperials, a pop gospel quartet. The Sweet Inspirations, a black trio of soul girls. Bobby Morris and the International's 35 musicians. Elvis' own band out in front of it all.

The huge room was buzzing. Voices. Brass. Strings. Laughter.

Larry Muhoberac was chasing some rock runs on the piano placed down in front. James Burton was inventing something on his lead guitar. Jerry Sheff on bass was driving some kind of music through his fingers. Ronny Tutt was making drum tuning sound like concert work. John Wilkerson was walking on with his rhythm guitar.

Elvis was the only entertainer who had brought a separate rock 'n roll band out front of his regular stage band. Great image.

It looked like a three ring circus. Elvis strolled out from the wings into the spotlight—the ringmaster of the circus and its star performer, all wrapped up in one person.

Glenn D. Hardin remembers the tremendous effort Elvis put into getting a show into shape. Glenn missed the Las Vegas opening but he came on with his piano, starting with the second engagement at the International.

Elvis would rehearse straight through the night sometimes. He worked as hard in rehearsals as he did in concert. You worked hard under Elvis.

When it looked like everybody had to have a break, I'd play the opening bars of the movie cartoon theme, "Looney Tunes."

Elvis would stop and smile and call out, "Let's take a break."

He drove us like musical maniacs but it was always fun with Elvis out front.

Elvis worked at breakneck speed but he always knew exactly what he wanted to happen on stage and where he was going.

He made things happen for us. He could change an entire

show with no more than a glance at us. He could grab music out of the stratosphere.

You kept your eyes on him or you fell off a fast moving train.

With Elvis in front of us, we were all better musicians.

Few people, certainly no one in the audience, ever knew as well as Glenn just how closely me and Elvis worked during a concert. Glenn could hear us talking.

Glenn's piano top was where I kept the list of show tunes I called out to Elvis and the stage band. It was where I kept Elvis' mineral water to sip during the show. It was where I leaned my guitar.

Charlie spent an awful lot of time on the show itself. Directing stage work. Picking the songs. Rehearsals. He even made his voice sound like Elvis' so he could help out with the high notes when Elvis got tired. Charlie could imitate Elvis' voice so well that the audience never knew it was Charlie's voice they were listening to if Elvis' faded.

When Elvis bowed his head to the applause you could see him turn his head toward Charlie when Charlie called out the name of the next song. If he wanted to change it, he'd go over and get a sip of water from Charlie, tell him what he wanted to sing next, then jump into it—and Charlie had the job of bringing the rest of us along. I always had to kick off those surprise changes.

You scrambled. You had to be on your toes with Elvis.

The Desert Explosion

By July 26, the show came together.

It was pure Elvis.

In the International Showroom that night, the Las Vegas audience smiled politely, then sat upright with a gasp and was blown out across the desert by an Elvis explosion.

The audience sat stunned when Elvis walked out on stage in his *gi* to the thundering beat of "That's All Right, Mama" without a single word of introduction. They jumped to their feet and clapped like crazy.

We couldn't start the show until after he had finished the first two songs. The audience was too uptight to sit back and relax and go with the flow.

After that night, we were never able to start an Elvis stage show until after a couple of opening songs had gone by. So, when he came out, I would place the strap of his guitar over his head. The band would keep on vamping. Then Elvis would go back to the middle of the stage and start singing, with the band behind him.

He'd sing a couple of songs, then hand the guitar back to me and sing, "Love Me."

He'd walk along the edge of the stage and let them look at him. He'd let them touch his hand. Let them watch him move about. He would kiss a couple of girls in the footlights.

He had to give the audience time to say, "Elvis is a real person. Not just a legend." Then they would slowly sit back and start breathing again. You could see it happening from the stage. Then you could go ahead with your regular show program.

It was a strange phenomenon. It was repeated at every show Elvis ever did, from then on.

Cary Grant came to one of the International shows and sat through it, wiping tears from his eyes. He came backstage afterward with Kirk Kerkorian, owner of the hotel and the MGM studios.

"Did you see Cary crying out there?" Kerkorian asked Elvis.

Elvis looked puzzled. He had not been able to see much at all through the heavy lights.

"Don't worry," Kerkorian said. "Cary cries at everything that is beautiful. Ballet. Paintings. Sculpture. Poetry. Elvis."

"Will you be taking your show on the road?" Cary asked.

"Yes, sir," Elvis said.

"Wonderful," Grant said. "More people should have a chance to see it."

"Thank you, sir."

Yul Brynner came up to Elvis' suite one night after a show.

There is a kind of giant-ness about the guy when you see him coming toward your through a crowd.

He came striding up to Elvis. He looked like the real King of Siam in a tux. People got quiet.

"Elvis," he boomed, in that deep and royal voice of his with the touch of some strange accent. "Thank you, for the ENORMOUS amount of pleasure you have given us this evening."

It made you feel like sinking down on one knee and kissing the extended hand of a monarch.

"You Invented The Best"

Sammy Davis was down front at a table one night, right after Elvis decided to throw the 2001 Space Odyssey theme into James Burton's rock 'n roll guitar and the big drums and the screaming trumpets in the hotel orchestra and all the flashing lights—when Elvis strolls out with a smile to open the show.

I was at home one afternoon when Elvis came roaring in to the driveway. He slammed the door of his Stutz and came trotting in. "I was driving around and I picked up that '2001 Space Odyssey' theme. It's fantastic. I want it in the opening."

The opening was a sensation. Sammy Davis jumped up and down and cheered. Backstage, after that show, Sammy said, "When they hit the big drums with that BOOM— BOOM—BOOM—BOOM I thought the Roman Legions were marching in.

"Man, you're not just the best. You invented the best."

Chuck Connors completely broke Elvis up when he came galloping into Elvis' suite one night after a show. He starred in television's "The Rifleman" series. He stands six feet and four inches tall. He came into the suite, just towering over us all.

He spotted Elvis and yelled across the room, "Elvis! You're not a *$A&N star. You're a *$A&N GALAXY!

Elvis was always thrilled to see Jack and Marie Lord fly in from Hawaii to see his show.

We were always a little surprised to see them through the footlights. They would catch the early show and then stay around the hotel to see the second one. They had such a heavy television filming schedule for their series, "Hawaii Five-O," that they usually tried to be in bed every night by eight o'clock at the latest.

Elvis always invited them to come up to his suite for a little private party. He loved those two. They returned the love.

Elvis always tried to do something special for them. Usually, it would include calling the Stamps Quartet and J.D. Sumner to come up to the suite and share some of his favorite gospel songs with the Lords.

Jack's hand, as they listened, would reach out and rest on Marie's hand.

Elvis always loved to see that kind of affection between a man and his wife.

A Thousand Echoes . . .

Elvis' desert explosion was repeated in hundreds of coliseums, arenas and auditoriums all across the country. From New York City's Madison Square Garden to the Forum in Los Angeles, the Omni in Atlanta, the Cow Palace in San Francisco, the Astrodome in Houston, the Mid-South Coliseum in Memphis.

We got so keyed up during those concerts that strange things sometimes happened to the audience and to us on stage.

One night, on tour, Elvis reached way back somewhere in him and uncorked an incredible show. The band and everyone on stage was on a big creative binge.

The audience was flying. They took the show even higher.

When it was over, the orchestra was doing the jungle beat "walk off music." Elvis was walking along the edge of the stage, shaking hands with people. He had begun to stand sideways so they couldn't grab his hand and yank him off the stage into the crowd.

Then he was heading off stage before people realized it.

I grabbed my jacket and tucked my music book of lyrics under my arm and headed off stage one way while Elvis was going off on the other side of the stage.

Jerry Schilling was down on the floor of the auditorium. He was at the edge of the stage that was about seven feet high.

"Hey, Charlie!" he yelled up at me over the noise. "Give me a hand up."

I reached down and grabbed his hand. I thought he was just going to walk up the side of the stage, using my hand to steady himself. After all, I wasn't that strong.

When I reached down to grab his hand, I looked back to see if Elvis needed any help, or what was going on with the body guards and the fans.

The place was in a uproar.

When I turned around, I nearly ran into Jerry on stage. He stood there beside me with a funny look on his face.

"Come on, boy," I yelled at him. "Let's go."

He was looking at me like a stranger. Sort of blank.

Back at the motel, I stood in front of the air conditioner to cool off.

"You know what you did?" Jerry said, filling a glass with ice.

"What are you talking about?" I said.

"Remember when I asked you to give me a hand up?" he said.

"Sure, Jerry."

"Well," he said, "you reached down, grabbed my hand and lifted me straight up and set me on the stage. I weigh 185 pounds, Charlie."

Elvis told me once, "Charlie, I believe there is some kind of great power locked inside us all. It's there when we need it."

Maybe I had picked up some of that power while I watched him touching the outstretched hands of people at the edge of the stage.

The Guitar Sailed Across The Stage . . .

You watched Elvis like a hawk during a show or you were in big trouble.

One night, he started doing his karate moves with his guitar.

At the end of his song he lunged at the audience with the guitar. He froze an instant. Then he straightened and flung the guitar backward over his shoulder. He didn't look where he threw it.

Someone in the audience screamed.

The guitar sailed across the stage like a baseball home run. Then it arched down through the air toward me. I jumped over a step to my right. I grabbed the guitar by the slender neck as it came down.

The audience was silent. No one moved. Then the audience let out a yell and started applauding and whistling.

Elvis turned around to me and smiled real big. Happy as a kid.

He had known I would be watching his every move. He knew I would grab his guitar before it could hit the floor. Now the audience knew it and Elvis got a kick out of that.

The Wild And Divine . . .

There was a wild and divinely unpredictable side of Elvis on stage that Glenn likes to remember:

Sometimes we called him Crazy—just as a nickname.
One night, during a show, he stopped everything to introduce his rock 'n roll band. He was proud of us. He

thought we were tops and he wanted the audience to know it.

Charlie always kept a glass of mineral water waiting for Elvis on top of my piano. Elvis wanted cold water. Charlie wouldn't let him have it. "Warm water is better for your voice, Elvis," Charlie kept saying.

That night, Elvis picked up the glass of water and sipped it. He made a face and slowly poured the rest of it over my head.

Everybody roared.

Charlie was scared. Really scared.

"Elvis, don't ever do that to James Burton," he said.

"How come?" Elvis asked.

"Because he has a whole lot of hot amps going through his electric guitar," Charlie said, quite seriously. "You would electrocute him on stage."

But Elvis was having too much fun with the thing to stop doing it.

I fooled him the next night, though. When he took a sip of the warm water, made a face and turned to me with the rest of it—I was waiting for him.

He lifted it and tilted it over my head.

As he poured, I snapped open a little umbrella.

Elvis broke up, laughing.

The guy could never really get mad at anyone on stage with him.

He was easy to work with—a breeze.

We were never so much alive as when we were with Elvis.

When something happened in a concert that he didn't like, he didn't just gloss over and go on. Elvis would stop the show, go back and do the thing right—then go on.

He knew how to make bad things actually work for him.

One night, at a concert, Ronnie did a crazy thing. It hurt the show, but Elvis managed to pull it out.

Elvis called for one of those dramatic numbers, the ones that built up to a big emotional close. Screaming brass and thundering drums.

He liked to throw his clenched fist at the sky to call for the final crashing beat of thundering drums.

Ronnie got a crazy idea. That night, when Elvis threw his fist up to the sky, Ronnie held up a little triangle and struck it.

Out came a prissy little tinkle.

The whole audience froze in silence.

Elvis turned and looked at Ronnie. He had that look we all called "the angry Elvis look."

Ronnie lowered the triangle. His face froze.

He had tried to be funny and it had gone horribly wrong.

Elvis turned back to the front of the stage. He threw his clenched fist at the sky once more.

You never heard such an explosion of Ronnie Tutt drums and screaming brass in a piercing, shattering final blast that rocked the whole building.

Then silence.

The audience roared and jumped to its feet.

Elvis waved and smiled.

Racing Down The Colorado Ski Slope...

A bright sun slid behind the stony Colorado mountain peaks. Darkness settled over the mountain shoulders.

Finally, the guys got back from Denver with the motorized sleds that Elvis had sent for.

Elvis said he wanted to ride them up to Lost Boy Ridge.

We had all gone up to the resort of Vail for a break. Elvis had a house up there. Some of the boys stayed with him. The rest of us rented condos.

It was a beautiful clear night for the climb. The skiiers had long since got off the snowy slopes. They were partying in warm pubs, in front of fireplaces or tucked away under thick blankets for the night.

We, of course, were just waking up.

By ten o'clock that night it was icy cold outside. I stuffed myself into some thick snowboots and gloves and heavy pants. I pulled on a downy coat with a heavy hood that would come down over my face. I was going to stay warm.

Elvis jumped into the lead motorized sled and we all started up the steep mountain.

There was a lot of security around Elvis. Jerry Kennedy, head of the Denver narcotics squad, had skiied these slopes many times. He knew the mountains. He knew his way through the dark, staying close to the regular ski trails. Elvis had Joe telephone Jerry and invite him up to join us, if he had some vacation time on the books.

"Tell him to bring some of the guys with him, if they have

135

some vacation time they want to spend with us," Elvis said. "Tell him, I'd love to have them."

So, some of the Denver police were making the climb with all of us.

On the dark slope, Elvis kept looking back over his shoulder. You could barely see little pinpoints of light in the village far below us. Like little stars.

Elvis loved it.

At the top of Lost Boy Ridge, Elvis turned his sled around. We fell in behind.

The view, starting back down, was breathtaking. So was the high altitude. It was what outer space must look like.

Then I noticed that my snowmobile was going faster than I wanted it to. I stomped the pedal that was supposed to slow the thing down. It didn't seem to make a bit of difference.

The sled kept picking up speed and the cold wind whistled off the tip of my nose. Every mound of snow made me bounce worse through the dark.

My stomach felt like I was going over the top of a hill and dropping down too fast on the other side.

The snowmobile was fixing to turn over.

I looked back. Joe was coming down right behind me.

He said, later, it looked like I finally just lifted off the side of the mountain like a man coming off a ski jump and sailed through the air.

I let go the snowmobile and shoved away from it. It came down again and bounced out of control and started tumbling down the hill. I was doing flips down the hill and it was right behind me.

Then the thing bounced high and came down in the snow on its two runners. It stuck there, its rear end pointed up at the stars.

I worked my way down the slope to it. I heaved the thing out of the snowbank and headed down the slope again. I caught up with everybody in the dark.

Their bobbing flashlights looked like lightning bugs riding skis.

Grandma's Egg Butter

A little before the snow turned blue in the early morning dawn, we were all sitting in front of the big fireplace in Elvis' house.

The hot fire made his cheeks pink.

"That mesquite wood makes a hot fire," he said, watching the flames.

I started telling him about how me and Lindalee would make Grandma's Egg Butter for everybody in the Nevada show on those cold mornings out there—and how good it tasted when you smeared it on hot biscuits at breakfast.

"How do you make Grandma's Egg Butter?" Elvis said, lighting a long thin cigar and tossing one across to a policeman who held up his hands for one.

"It sounds like this is a real good night for some of that stuff." He told one of the other policemen, "Look in that drawer over there and get you a cigar. Pass them out."

"Well, it's made out of eggs and butter with some sugar," I said.

"How much?" he said.

"I don't remember, Elvis. Not the exact recipe, anyway. Wish I did."

"Call Lindalee and get the recipe for it," he said.

"Now?" I asked.

"Yea, now," he said. "What's wrong with now?" He picked up the phone and tossed it to me. "Go ahead."

It was four o'clock in the morning. It was still pitch black on the mountains out the window.

I got out my little phone book.

Lindalee would understand.

She remembers the call like this:

I was still asleep when my hand picked up the phone.

Charlie said, "Lindalee, honey, Elvis is up here at Vail. In deep snow. I told him what we needed was some of your

Grandma's Egg Butter. He threw me a phone and said to get the recipe and make him a batch."

Elvis picked up another phone. He still remembered Lindalee's Oakie Fudge. Now he was going to have some of her Grandma's Egg Butter.

"Lindalee," he said, "I want you to bring your folks and all come down to Vegas to see our next show. You can stay at the International with us."

We got to talking about the old days when Charlie worked with Daddy. How Charlie would try to crack me up when we were on stage together. He'd cross his eyes at me while he sang a love ballad and slip his hand behind me and unzip my dress in back.

The only way I could get back at him was to eat a whole onion right before going on stage and breathing heavy in his eyes. It nearly knocked him off the stage. But he kept right on smiling and singing through the fumes.

Elvis asked me down to Las Vegas one time before. When I got there, I went up to the gorgeous suite he had waiting for me. I looked at myself in a full-length mirror on one wall and said, "No, sir, I'm not wearing blue jeans and sneakers in the main room tonight. Tonight, I'm going to be glamorous."

I tried on a really gorgeous gown with a neckline that plunged all the way down to my waist. I screwed on some big loop earrings. I brushed up my hair. Then came the special makeup.

I stood back and looked at myself again. I was ready.

The show was moving fast when they seated me right at the edge of the stage. It was all big brass and kettle drums and Elvis slapping a thigh and sharp bits of light bouncing off his jumpsuit, big rings covering his hand and Charlie watching him with a big smile.

Elvis came by my table and looked down at me funny and kept moving. He kissed some girls at the next table. He flipped a scarf at a woman and looked at me again in a strange way. A big old Texan at the next table stood up and put his hand over his heart in salute during the American Trilogy at the end.

Going off stage, with the fast tempo finale, Elvis looked back at me again and then he was gone. I looked up and Charlie was signalling me to get upstairs fast.

Elvis was lying on a huge couch in his suite by the time I got up there.

"Wakely, is that you?" he asked.

I nodded. "Did I bother your act tonight? Sorry, if I did."
He shook his head.

"That wasn't it," he said. "In those footlights, all dressed up, you made me think of Priscilla. She took Lisa Marie and went back to Memphis on the plane this afternoon. I was wondering, 'What is Priscilla doing back here?'"

When he looked at me through the lights, he had seen Priscilla and the image had driven him nuts.

He Felt Safer On A Horse

Elvis' favorite getaway place was back home.

Fans were always down at the front gate at Graceland. At night they gathered to watch the lights go on and off in the different rooms.

Some nights, Elvis would call out to the barn and have Mike McGregor saddle up Rising Sun so he could ride down to the gate and sign autographs and talk. He felt safer on a horse.

One night he called down to the gate. His Uncle Harold Lloyd was on duty down there.

"Open the gate," Elvis said. "Tell the fans to come inside."

"Come inside?" Harold echoed.

"Just hold on," Elvis said. "Tell them to come on inside. then shut the gate after them and lock it."

"Lock 'em inside?" Harold echoed again.

"That's right," Elvis said.

So Harold opened the gate and the fans came on inside. They looked up at the mansion, expecting to see Elvis coming out the front door.

A car honked behind them in the street.

They turned around. It was Elvis, driving along the boulevard, smiling and waving at them.

They all ran back to the gate. It was shut. Elvis drove on out of sight.

They didn't know what to do.

Then they saw Elvis' car swing in the back gate. Elvis got out and walked down the winding driveway toward them. They were so stunned they didn't move.

They dissolved when he walked in among them and smiled.

"Hi, gang."

He Played Games With The Fans . . .

Elvis played games with fans at the gate.

Sometimes he played games even with his own guards.

His Uncle Vester worked as security on the front gate for 15 years. He tried to keep the fans from overrunning the grounds but sometimes they were able to get around his flanks, especially when it got dark. No matter how careful he was.

This is what he said happened to him one night when he was on duty all by himself:

There were seven or eight cute girls giving me more trouble than usual that night.

All of a sudden, they came over the wall. I yelled. They scattered in the dark and ran up the hill screaming.

Oh, I was hot. I took out after them in the dark. I couldn't see anything at all. Then it got real quiet. I couldn't hear a thing. They were being awful quiet somewhere.

Then I heard some whispering back in the hedges, up near the house.

I went over there and yelled, "All right, girls. I know you're hiding back in there. Just come on out."

Nothing happened. I heard some more giggling.

"You girls better come on out if you know what's good for you," I said.

Well, about that time, I heard Elvis' voice coming out of the hedges.

"Leave them alone, Uncle Vester," he said. "I'm back in here with them."

*Elvis would never say anything or do anything to put
someone down. He always made everyone feel they were a
part of it all. No matter how they dressed.*

He had a temper but he never turned it on you.

*One night he bought a new white Riviera and drove it up
to the front gate and honked. Nobody opened the gate to let
him drive in.*

*Harold Lloyd was on the gate that night and had walked
up the hill to check the house. Elvis thought Harold was
asleep in the gatehouse. So he just floorboarded the Riviera*

But Elvis never said a word to his Uncle Harold.

Elvis loved to watch Lisa Marie playing around Graceland.

One of her favorite games was to race the golf carts over
the little hills and across the pasture behind the mansion,
scattering the horses in front of her.

She would race the carts up and down the driveway in
front of the mansion with the fans craning their necks over
the stone wall to watch and wave.

One of the yard men told Elvis one day, "You had better
speak to her about racing that thing. She's going to get hurt
one of these days."

"Well, she's going to have to learn those things for herself,
sooner or later," Elvis said.

Lisa Marie had a way of bugging Elvis that he never did
get on top of.

She would start calling him Al-vis instead of Elvis. He
would try to correct her. Patiently.

"It's El-vis, honey. Not Al-vis. You can say that."

She would try again and make the same "mistake." She
knew what she was doing.

A Pony For Lisa . . .

One day somebody left a Shetland pony down at the front
gate with Uncle Harold. It had a pretty bridle and saddle. It
looked like it would be just right for Lisa Marie who didn't
have a horse but wanted one.

I walked down to the gate and looked at the pony.

"Harold, would you take a hundred dollars for it?" I said.

He grinned. "You got the money on you?"

I led the pony around to the barn and told Mike to look after it.

"I think it's going to be Lisa Marie's," I said.

"Pretty little thing," Mike said, taking the reins.

That afternoon, when Elvis woke up, I went upstairs to his office.

"What's up?" he said, yawning.

"I just bought a little Shetland, bridle, saddle and all," I said. "It's for Lisa Marie—if that's all right with you."

After he had breakfast, we walked out to the barn. Mike was brushing her and making her sparkle.

We leaned against a railing and watched. Elvis reached out and gently stroked a smooth neck.

"She's going to love it," he said. "Thanks, Charlie."

"But you still are the one to give it to her," I said.   'It's not for me to give her a pony. That's for her Daddy."

Elvis smiled.

Tough Girls at Palm Springs . . .

A couple of real tough girls hung out at our front gate in Palm Springs. They came close to ruining the place for Elvis.

Driving into Palm Springs, late at night, Elvis usually could look up in the rear view mirror and see them following him. He'd say, "They're back there."

You could be miles out of town and they would fall in behind Elvis' car.

The speedometer on Elvis' limousine would be reading at least 70. The girls would inch up closer and closer behind us. Near the back bumper so they could look right in the back window of the car.

Priscilla would hold Lisa Marie and ask Elvis if he could do something.

Joe, in the front seat, would grab the car telephone and call the highway patrol.

As soon as the girls saw the flashing lights of the highway patrol swing in behind us on the open highway, they would drop back to a safe distance. When the patrol car pulled alongside them, there was nothing that could be done. The girls would not be tailgating, at that point.

As soon as Elvis crossed into the Palm Springs city limits, Joe would call the city police for help.

One night, a Palm Springs policeman named Dick Grob heard Joe call for help.

Dick trailed the two girls a way and then hit them with his blue light and siren.

Dick pulled the girls over to the curb. He bathed their car in the spotlight. He got out of his car and walked up in a very imposing way. He had been in the first graduating class at the Air Force Academy. He had a commanding air about him.

He began by telling the girls that Palm Springs police had a tip that two girls were making heavy narcotics deals in town. He told them to get out of their car. To wait at the curb.

They got out. While they stared in disbelief, Dick took their car apart. He took out the seats. He emptied the trunk in the grass. He dumped out the glove compartment contents. He went through everything, even the ash trays in the back seat. He tossed floor mats on the grass.

"Good God," the dark haired girl said. "We're Elvis fans. How come you're taking the whole car apart?"

"We can't be too careful," Dick growled. "Sorry."

When he was sure we were safely inside our compound he'd let them go on their way.

Later in the night, when Elvis went out for a stroll around the grounds in the dark, the two girls were back at the front gate.

They watched. They waited.

Like a pair of cats at a mouse hole.

That kind of thing worried Elvis.

He looked around and found another hacienda in Palm Springs that he thought would give the family more security. He wrote a check for it.

There was a big swimming pool. Standing by it you could look up and see the mountains in the distance to the north.

It was huge.

One weekend, Elvis had a bunch of friends in from Los Angeles. Priscilla had gone back up to Los Angeles for some reason.

Folks were sitting around in the big living room, gawking and talking.

Elvis strolled in. Everything came to a halt until Elvis started up a new line of conversation.

As usual, Elvis soon was talking about the Bible. He started telling everybody one of his favorite Bible stories.

He kept feeling that he had a call to the ministry in some way but people kept talking him out of it.

Rex Humbard came to see him one night in Las Vegas. "Elvis," the great evangelist said, "stay with what you are doing. Your love of gospel music and your influence from the stage helps evangelism more than anything else I can think of."

The thought of entering the ministry, however, stuck in Elvis' mind.

He had a fantastic memory. He could quote religion books of all kinds, by the pages.

When he talked about religion he could be very dramatic. He did everything with enthusiasm, sometimes too much enthusiasm.

He'd get caught up in a story he was telling and he would come out with rough words he didn't mean to use.

So, that afternoon in Palm Springs, Elvis came in and started telling the girls in the living room a favorite Bible story. It was about the night in the garden of Gethsemane, just hours before Jesus died. That night had always been a very dramatic night in Elvis' mind.

Telling it, now, Elvis stood in front of the big picture window with the mountains in the background. Behind him was the pool. Beyond, in the valley below, lay Palm Springs. It was a beautiful backdrop for Elvis.

From time to time, he poked the air with an 18th Century jeweled walking stick. He had bought it at a Beverly Hills shop before leaving to drive to Palm Springs. It was beautiful.

The girls watched as if they were hypnotized.

"And so Jesus went to the garden that night," Elvis said intensely. "He took all his guys with him, one of whom was Peter.

"And Jesus said to Peter, 'You're going to have to look out for the Romans. They're on my case bad, tonight.'

"And Peter said, 'Don't sweat it, Jesus. I'll look out for the Romans. You just go ahead and do your thing.'"

I was sitting on a big couch, watching him. I picked up a pillow and held it in front of my face. I was about to laugh and I didn't want him to see me smiling.

Then Elvis heard Jerry Schilling break out with a laugh in the dining room. He frowned and walked to the entrance of the dining room and said, "Will you guys go outside with that stuff? I can't hear myself think."

They all got up silently and trooped out.

Elvis came back and continued with his story.

I had seen a lot of different Bible translations, from King James to Charlie Brown, but none compared with the Elvis manner of telling a Bible story.

Elvis had always been deeply moved by the lonely situation Jesus found himself in on that night in the garden. Jesus' disciples would fall asleep on him when he went apart into the trees to pray. They would not stay awake to watch for the soldiers. Peter would end up denying three times that he even knew Jesus.

Elvis got wrapped up in the story and it came out a bit

differently. Standing there with his feet spread wide apart, he swept the jeweled cane through the air. His face was full of history.

"Then Jesus said, 'Peter, you will fall asleep three times on me before the rooster crows.'

"And man, it made Peter hot. Peter said, 'No way, Lord. No way I'll fall asleep on you.'

"Jesus said, 'We'll see.'"

Elvis raised the jeweled cane and pointed it across the room at one of the girls sitting transfixed on the couch.

"And Jesus was dead right," he said. "It wasn't another 15 minutes before a bunch of Roman soldiers with torches marched in with Judas and they got his ass."

We all sat, silent as stone. No one dared laugh.

I got up and hurried outside and fell in the grass. "What's going on?" Jerry said, shaking me and trying to make me quit laughing. "What happened? Talk. Talk."

That night, the guys were sitting around the living room, laughing about what Elvis had said. Everybody got quiet and we looked at each other with straight faces when Elvis walked in.

Elvis glanced around at our solemn faces and strolled out. The chuckles started up again and died once more when Elvis came back in the room and looked at us.

"All right," Elvis said. "What's going on in here?"

We had to tell him.

When we got to the punch line, he slapped his forehead with an open palm and gasped, "Oh, my sweet Lord!"

Then he went outside and fell in the grass and lay there laughing, looking up at the desert stars.

Sometimes It Got Lonesome . . . . .

Sometimes during the engagements in Las Vegas, it could get lonesome. Even a place like that, where you wouldn't expect to find loneliness.

One night, one of the guys—who shall remain nameless—got to missing his wife. He drank too much. He went in to the restaurant and sat down and ordered a toasted cheese sandwich.

While he was waiting, he got a piece of paper and started to write his wife a love letter.

We found him like that—and walked him up to his room.

"I'll finish this later," he said and picked up the toasted cheese sandwich and put it in an inside jacket pocket.

In the hallway he said, "I better go ahead and mail this before I forget it." He pulled out the sandwich, walked over to a mail chute and stuffed the sandwich through its door.

Sometimes Elvis gambled a little, just to pass a little time, but he didn't care much for it.

But one night he happened to drop a silver dollar in one of the slot machines in the casino—and hit the $100 jackpot.

He kept feeding the thing silver dollars and it kept kicking out a jackpot every few turns.

The pit bosses got upset because there was no way they could make Elvis stop playing the busted machine.

A half dozen casino workers were standing around cracking their knuckles, just waiting for Elvis to walk away long enough for them to grab it.

Elvis came upstairs, laughing about it.

We rushed downstairs to see if the machine was still there.

The casino people had it loaded on a dolly hauling it out.

"Oh, Lord, My God..."

Elvis kept changing up the show. Surprising everybody. Making it better.

We were driving through the citrus country of California one day, heading for the next concert hall in our first tour of the state.

Joe and Jerry usually rode in the limousine with Elvis and his security, Red and Sonny. I rode in a trailing limousine with Linda Thompson, Dr. Nichopolous and a couple of other guys.

But on this particular day, I was riding with Elvis. He leaned over the back of the seat and said something about gospel music on stage.

I looked out my window. We were rolling fast through lemon orchards. You could smell the citrus in the warm air. Fresh and sharp.

We were due on a concert stage in less than 15 minutes.

"Charlie, let's put 'How Great Thou Art' in the show." Elvis said, sliding back in his seat. "Today."

Just like that.

"Hold it," I said. "I'm the only one up there on stage, besides you, that knows how you do that one."

"Then you just go over to the piano and do it," Elvis said, sliding his hat down over his eyes, faintly smiling.

As soon as we got to the auditorium I jumped out and ran inside and found The Imperials, the Sweet Inspirations and the boys in Elvis' band that worked out front on the stage.

"Elvis wants 'How Great Thou Art' in the show today," I said. "This is how we'll arrange it."

I turned to Glenn. "Glenn, you'll have to get up and let me sit down at the piano and get us into it. The rest of you can watch me and I'll cue you where to come in."

I hummed through the arrangement for them. They nodded. I showed them where they each came in and what they would do. Where the Sweet Inspirations would come in to make that big choir sound that Elvis would want to create around him.

Then it was showtime and we had to just wing it.

The show was rolling hard and fast and Elvis was like a surfer, skimming along on waves of applause coming in off the auditorium.

"Charlie," he said.

I looked at him.

He pointed at the piano. "Charlie, put down your guitar and go over to the piano."

I put down my guitar by the drums. Glenn got up from his piano and made room for me. I sat down and waited.

With no warning at all, Elvis turned back to the audience and sang the soft and lovely opening phrase, "Oh, Lord, my God ..."

My hands went to the keyboard. Fingers moved across it. Inside me, I heard the echoes. They came from a thousand gospel singing nights with the Pathfinders and the Foggy River Boys, with the Griggs sisters and all those Sunday afternoons with the youth choir back home in Decatur, harmonizing around the piano in Bad Nauheim and playing the smoky desert saloons with Jimmy Wakely.

Chords rose in my heart with notes flashing as clear as bird songs in early morning sunrise on the desert.

In a series of little miracles, everyone followed my piano cues as if they had worked for months on it. Elvis reached into the clouds for the phrasing as if God had created it and left it for him there to use that night on that stage. At the close, there was celestial thunder ringing from my keyboard.

Walking back to pick up my guitar again, I did not feel my feet touching the floor.

For the next three nights, I played the piano for the hymn. Glenn stood there and watched and then he took over. Joe Guercio was getting down key lines on his orchestration sheet. Joe directed the Las Vegas Hilton orchestra after directing for Edie Gorme and Steve Lawrence for 11 years. Elvis was the only entertainer the hotel would let Joe go out with. Not even Sinatra could get him to direct a tour, one time.

Every night, like some kind of wild flower, the great old hymn just grew and grew while we raced along on the tour.

Everyone was turned on, seeing a big new number take shape on stage while the show swept across the landscape at full tilt.

"I Split My Pants..."

You never knew what was going to happen on Elvis' show. Every show was different.

One night Elvis split his pants on stage.

He smiled at the audience. "I just split my pants," he said.

They wondered what on earth he would do.

So did we.

Elvis strolled over to the curtain, cool as you please. He pulled it up in front of him. Only his face was left showing. He kept right on talking about the show and the people in it.

Meanwhile behind the curtain, some of the guys were taking off his torn pants and putting on new ones.

When Elvis dropped the curtain and walked back out to center stage he had on new pants—and he never missed a lick.

The audience went crazy. With them, Elvis could do no wrong.

I hated to break the news to Elvis. It wasn't the kind of thing he liked to hear.

"The Imperials say they can't make the next tour," I told him when we started working on some new music for an upcoming tour.

"Why not?" he said.

"They have a contract with Jimmy Dean to do a tour with him," I said.

Elvis didn't like sudden changes like that.

The Imperials had missed a couple of other tours, in the same way.

"Let's just find us someone else for the show," Elvis said. "Find somebody who will stay with me."

Colonel Parker's office in Los Angeles sent over four singers. The first time Elvis heard them work was in the middle of a stage show. He listened and turned away and made a sour face. He strolled over to his sound control man, Felton Jarvis.

"Turn them down," he said. "Leave the female voices up."

Felton was sitting by the man who was operating the sound console.

After we came back in off the tour, Tom Diskin called from the Colonel's office.

"I heard Elvis didn't like the quartet," he said.

"Mr. Diskin, the four guys can sing but they don't make what we call a quartet," I said.

"I see," Tom said. "Well, you find the quartet."

"Well, I can call some people," I said.

"Right. See what you can do. You don't have much time before you open in Minneapolis."

"Right."

I thought of J.D. Sumner who had the Stamps Quartet. I had known him since he sang with the Sunshine Boys across the South before coming out to Hollywood to make budget movies with the Durango Kid.

His voice rumbled through the telephone line from Nashville when I caught him at home.

"Yea, Charlie," he said. "I'd love for my boys to sing on Elvis' show. Have you heard them? They're all youngsters."

"Have you got anything out on records on them?" I said.

"Yea. I got a brand new album," he said.

I asked him to send it out to the Colonel's office at MGM in Hollywood. I wanted Tom Diskin to know what a real quartet sounded like.

A couple of days later, Tom called. He asked me to come right over to his office.

The album was on their turntable when I walked in. They were all gathered around it, listening to J.D. singing with the quartet, going way, way down, rumbling those low notes that made the water in a glass flutter.

Elvis was wearing those dark rimmed glasses of his when I took the album over for him to listen to. He was reading a book on religion.

I put the album on for him. He listened to it all the way through—just because he loved that kind of singing.

"Can we get them in time for Minneapolis?" he said.

I went over to his desk and called J.D. at home in Nashville. When he picked up the phone I said, "Elvis wants you guys to open with him in Minneapolis."

"I don't see how we can do it," J.D. answered after a long pause. "The quartet is out on the road now. You'll be pulling in to Minneapolis to start the tour just about the moment my boys will be coming back in off the road. They won't be able to get together for a single rehearsal before you open, Charlie."

The key to the whole thing was going to be J.D.'s remarkable nephew, Donny, who played piano, sang and was master of ceremonies for the quartet on the road.

Donny was simply a genius.

"We're all going down to Palm Springs for a few days, "I told him. "Let me give you the phone number down there. Have Donny call me tonight after they come off stage, wherever they are. We'll talk it out on the phone. I can tell them where they come in and what their musical cues will be. I can put the phone on my piano and play it for them. Then they can try it out. I can listen on the phone until it starts to sound right."

Elvis got restless in Palm Springs after only a couple of days. He decided to fly back to Memphis. He wanted to spend a few days at Graceland before leaving on the new tour. He flew out that afternoon.

I stayed on in the desert by myself. I worked nights on the phone with Donny and the quartet. Every night they called from a new place on the tour.

A couple of days before we were to open in Minneapolis, I called Joe at Graceland.

"Are you still down in Palm Springs?" he asked. He sounded surprised.

"Yea, but I'm flying out to Nashville tonight," I said. "The Stamps are coming off the road late tonight. They ought to get at least one good rehearsal with me before coming on stage with Elvis' show in Minneapolis. So, we'll meet the rest of you in Minneapolis in time for the opening."

"You're cutting it thin," Joe said.

"It's okay," I said.

I flew to Nashville. The next morning I drove downtown. I met the boys in the quartet at a rehearsal studio Felton Jarvis got for me through his people at RCA.

"Where's J.D.?" I asked when I walked in.

"Oh, he's out of town," Donny said. "But he'll be here in time to ride along with us in the morning."

"Ride along?" I said. "Elvis wants J.D. singing with the quartet when we open tomorrow in Minneapolis."

Danny looked alarmed. "He thought Elvis just wanted him to come along for company."

"He has to sing," I said. "You'll have to get together with him as soon as our plane lands in Minneapolis to go through it with him."

I forgot the time.

Felton came in the studio from his office just down the hall. He glanced at the wall clock.

"Charlie," he said, "do you realize you have been on your feet, rehearsing for the past six hours? You were supposed to be at Lamar Fike's house for supper 30 minutes ago. He just called to see if I knew where you were."

I felt high—but worn out.

I found my pack of cigarets under the sheet music on top of the piano and lit one. I went through my jacket pockets and dug out the plane tickets.

"Here are your tickets," I said. "It sounds good, Donny. See you guys at the airport. We'll open in Minneapolis tomorrow night."

When I got back to the hotel I called Joe at Graceland.

"Joe, my stage wardrobe is still packed from the last tour," I said. "It's in my room. Make sure they put it on the plane in the morning. Otherwise, I won't have a thing to wear."

"Sounds daring," he said. Joe, the joker.

My guitar would be waiting for me on stage when I walked on, tomorrow night. It would be tuned. Somebody would take care of that. Because that was the kind of organization Elvis had. Eighty-eight people could move across the country with no sweat, the Colonel had it organized so well.

When J.D. got back to Nashville, late that night, he got me on the phone.

"Why does Elvis need me to sing?" he said. "The quartet already has a bass. A good one."

"Elvis feels that two bass singers would help him get the choir sound behind him that he likes on stage," I said.

He thought about it. "The boy does have nice ideas."

"Minneapolis thinks so," I said. "We're all sold out."

The next afternoon in Minneapolis, we had just enough time before the show for a quicky rehearsal of the parts of the show that used the vocal groups.

In the show, when J.D. started those vocal rumblings like an erupting volcano, Elvis got a sip of mineral water at Glenn's piano top and asked me, "Any trouble getting J.D. to come in?"

I kept smiling. "None, Elvis."

He nodded and ambled off toward the microphone.

He knew.

He raised one hand and brought the show to an unexpected halt.

"Ladies and gentlemen," he said. "I'd like to introduce the members of the show. Let's start with Mr. J.D. Sumner and his Stamps Quartet."

There was applause.

"J.D., it's good working on the same stage with you," Elvis said. He turned back to the audience. "When I was a kid and couldn't afford a ticket, J.D. always let me in the back door at those gospel quartet shows that came through.

"Now I'm coming through the front door and bringing in J.D. with me."

Elvis always played to J.D. on his side of the stage and me on mine. That way, Elvis was always playing to a friend who was up there urging him on.

And when Elvis went to the National Quartet Convention in Nashville, J.D. made a special little booth for him to sit in and listen—so that his presence would not be known and upset the performance. J.D. operated the convention and sponsored it.

Laughter Surrounds Elvis

There was a lot of joy and laughter around Elvis.

When Elvis laughed, it was impossible not to feel an irresistible urge to laugh yourself. He loved to laugh. His laughter was infectious. And it helped us get through some long and weary nights.

Strangely, one of his biggest hit recordings in Europe, four long years after he left us all, was a 1970 recording of Elvis—laughing his way through the song "Are You Lonesome Tonight?"

We were on the stage at the International Hotel,

Having fun on stage, by clowning around,
Elvis with a guitar pick in his mouth.

recording a live performance. Elvis decided to change up the words of the song. Where the real lines go, "Do you gaze at your doorstep and picture me there," Elvis substituted, just for fun, "Do you gaze at your bald head and wish you had hair."

After he did that he started laughing. He couldn't get the idea out of his mind. Or the bald image. He finally got tickled and laughing so hard that it began breaking up the rest of the cast.

Everybody on stage began sliding into a laughing binge. Elvis looked around for help but there wasn't any to be found. He carried a guitar pick in his hand to press the sharp point into his palm. The pain usually helped him regain control, no matter what. But the pick didn't help this time.

Everywhere he looked on stage, there was someone else laughing. He finally went to pieces. It was hilarious.

On the record you can hear him gasp, "Fourteen years right down the tube with that one song."

Only one person on the huge Showroom stage still had any sort of control. It was Sissy of the Sweet Inspirations. She was still "oooo-ing" along, doing a nice backup for the song that Elvis was supposed to be singing.

Elvis looked over at Sissy through the tears and said, "Sing it, baby!"

Sometime, when you're feeling blue, listen to Elvis laughing.

It'll make you feel good in no time at all.

The Two Drunks

Two drunks sat with their wives at a table at the edge of the stage one night during an Elvis concert at the International Hilton Showroom.

They were making nasty remarks. They loudly announced they liked Tom Jones better than Elvis. Things like that. It was making their wives mad.

Elvis in his Las Vegas dressing room with
"Master Rhee"...

It was also making a little guy named Kang Rhee mad.

Kang Rhee had flying fists and feet. A master of TaeKwonDo karate, he taught the art to Korean Army intelligence officers for two years before coming to Memphis to set up his own school.

Elvis studied with Master Rhee. He took him on some of his concert tours. It was an amazing experience for Master Rhee who tells what happened in Las Vegas when the two drunks tried to heckle Elvis.

His story goes like this:

Elvis stop show and walk over to the two guys and say something real rough to them.

The audience cheer and clap.

I go over to their table. I tap the two guys on shoulder. When they look at me they swallow hard and say, "You Elvis' karate teacher?"

I say, "It don't matter. You in trouble. See you after concert over."

They got up and ran out.

After concert, I go to dressing room. Elvis say, "A waiter say some little Oriental scare those two guys away. That must be you."

He call Charlie Hodge and he appear in room.

"Write Master Rhee check for thousand dollars," Elvis say.

I didn't want him to do that. But Elvis say take it or he be mad with me.

Other fans bother Elvis in Pittsburgh. Before he can get out and go in hotel, they surround Elvis' car. He can't get out.

I jump out and stare at crowd. I yell, "Ki-Hop!" It's a karate cry. I stomp my foot and took a karate position with tension.

Fans stop screaming and shoving. They look at me. They move back. Elvis jump out and got into hotel door.

There was a big fan party for Elvis after Atlanta show. Lots of food. In a big hotel there.

One lady wrote poem to Elvis. She read it.

Elvis called Lowell Hays, who make jewelry for him, to bring his big jewel box. He pick out big diamond ring and give woman.

He never knew her before. She is a stranger. So it is not a personal thing.

So I see that he gives away jewels to entertain people.

Always he is the entertainer.

He gave all the women rings.

Elvis' greatest gift was his friendship, George Klein always said.

George got such a gift from Elvis, one night in Las Vegas.

Elvis, with a play on words, said I played the key part in it.

George tells about that night like this:

You can wreck a gift of a car. You can lose gift jewelry. Clothes you can hang in a closet and forget. But when a man gives you a nice wedding, that becomes a real part of you—from then on.

Elvis gave me a wedding.

Until that night, he had never even been a best man at anybody's wedding.

He called me one night from California. It was December. He wanted to fly me and Barbara Little, Dr. Nichopolous' nurse, out to Las Vegas. He wanted us to get married in his Imperial Suite at the Hilton.

"I've always loved you," he said. "You and Barbara. Your life, Your future. I know I waited a long time to make up my mind. I think it's time we all did this. It's the best thing."

He talked to me like a brother.

So we flew out there.

His Imperial Suite was beautifully decorated for the wedding. At one big window was an archway of flowers. The lights of Las Vegas twinkled through it.

Elvis stood on one side of the archway and I stood on the other with the Rabbi beside me. Barbara and Dr. Nick were in the adjoining room getting ready.

Charlie was kidding around.

So Elvis said, "Charlie, knock off the comedy. Go over to the piano and get ready to play the Wedding March."

So Charlie sat down and started thumping out the Wedding March. Just practicing it.

Elvis looked around and yelled, "Not yet, Charlie!"

Too late.

Dr. Nick and Barbara heard Charlie on the Wedding March and they thought that was their cue. They started marching in to Charlie's beat.

So Charlie had to keep on playing.
But it really turned out to be beautiful.
It was a wonderful gift.

One Of His Crazy Ideas...

One night, at a concert, Elvis wanted to slow down the pace of the show a little.

He began singing a quiet ballad.

I was standing beside him, holding a microphone up for his voice. He was sitting on a stool, playing his guitar. Resting. The stand mike was at the hole in his guitar.

He had a baby spotlight on his face.

In a low and seductive voice he sang, "Are You Lonesome Tonight?"

He got a crazy idea, halfway through the song.

Elvis' big blue eyes started drifting over in my direction. I saw it coming.

I decided to play the same game and bounce it back into his court.

I put the flat palm of my hand up and carefully stroked it over my hair.

As he continued in that low seductive voice of his, I lowered my eyelids until they were dreamily half shut, warm and limpid. I let a lambent smile begin to flutter and play around the corners of my mouth.

I tried to look as gay as I could.

That switch took Elvis by surprise. He cracked up, almost shy. The audience loved it.

"Stop it, Charlie," he said, off mike. "This is the kind of town where people are going to believe anything about you."

He kept laughing and trying to sing and we finally got through to the end and the audience tore up the house with applause. The thing had worked and we now had a comedy act for Elvis' show whenever he wanted to relax a few minutes.

Me 'n Elvis...

Are You Lonesome...

Tonight?

I looked around at Glenn and said, "'Teddy Bear.'" He nodded.

"It's going to be 'Teddy Bear'," I told Elvis, with nobody else hearing me. "Tell Glenn when you're ready to kick it off."

He paused to wipe tears of laughter out of his eyes. He handed me his guitar and pointed a finger at Glenn. That finger sent a whole new tide of music rolling across the stage with the easy feeling of a well oiled show with a super star effortlessly handling the controls.

Keeping up with Elvis on stage was exhausting. He had a driving power that never let up. He moved to the music. He was a person of great dynamism. Working alongside him took all the energy we had.

One night, after we had just come back from a long tour, I was worn out and still on an emotional high—so high that I had trouble sleeping.

Without some rest, I was going to be a blithering basket case. Fit for nothing or nobody—on stage or off.

Dr. Nichopolous had given me something new that day in an effort to end my insomnia. It was a hypnotic, not the usual thing that works on the central nervous system.

The thing hit me while I was standing up in the bathroom, getting ready to go to bed. I crashed straight forward, onto the linoleum rug, face first.

Elvis and Priscilla heard it and came running in. Elvis had a gun in one hand and a long flashlight in the other. He thought I might be a burglar.

He picked me up and put me in bed. He stuffed pillows behind me to make me sit up and not fall asleep. He told me I had to stay awake. The pill was a hypnotic so I did everything he said do.

Priscilla got some wet cloths. They washed the blood off my face.

There was a lot of blood where I hit my nose on the rug. Elvis got my mouth open and looked up in there with his long flashlight.

Sometimes I felt sure that Elvis' life was going to kill me.

At the same time, I also felt quite sure that Elvis Presley would never die.

That special smile...

The Laughter Changes

One day, something happened to the laughter.

I felt that it had changed. There was a new tone to it. A little sad, maybe.

Ray Walker, big bass singer for the Jordanaires, noticed it. He saw the change in Elvis one day in the RCA recording studios in Nashville:

Elvis was sitting backward in one of those cane chairs in the studio when I came in. I hadn't seen him since he opened in Las Vegas in 1969. He had heard some wrong reasons about why we had decided not to go with him to Las Vegas.

The real story was that we had begun to get so many recording dates after we started making those movies with Elvis that we couldn't afford to leave Nashville.

Elvis saw me walk into the RCA studio. He jumped over the back of his chair and a railing and ran to me. He put his long arms under mine and nearly picked me up. He seemed so glad to see me.

I said, "Elvis, we wish we could have been with you all these years. But we had so much going on here in Nashville. And our kids were coming along and we didn't want to be away from them all the time."

Elvis said, "Now, don't you worry about that. I just wish I had that good a reason not to go out on the road so much."

Elvis loved being on the road. It was just that he missed his family.

Priscilla and Lisa Marie were gone by then. That's what Elvis meant.

There was so much about his life that he never could understand. Sometimes he got so frustrated with things that he would tremble with anger.

But he never hurt anybody. Elvis never could.

During some long nights he would do a lot of yelling on the phone, yet he never touched a living soul.

He made many bitter threats, and ended up wondering how he might help the person he threatened.

That was Elvis' way.

One night, after one of those emotional storms had passed he said, "Charlie, I'm not going to hurt anybody. I just have to have some way to get it out of my system. Otherwise, I'll go crazy."

There were many lonely nights like that. All you could do for him then was just sit up with him and listen.

There were many friends around him.

We gave him all that he needed but the one most important thing of all, that special kind of love that only comes from a woman.

Others like to describe things differently, but that is the way it was.

The Laughter Changed...

The laughter kept changing.

One night during a show in Las Vegas someone started throwing Teddy Bears up on the stage at Elvis. They were falling all around him.

Elvis laughed and scooped them up and threw them back out at the audience. It got to be a big game, throwing the Teddy Bears back and forth. The audience loved it.

One of the Teddy Bears hit a beautiful cousin of his in the audience. She was sitting at one of the tables with her wealthy husband. They liked to fly out to see Elvis perform. Elvis dearly loved her.

Well, when he grabbed up one of the Teddy Bears and threw it back at the audience, it hit his cousin's wig and knocked it off her head. She looked funny as hell. It cracked up the whole showroom. His cousin just howled with laughter.

It wasn't long after that when Elvis got a phone call.

It was some of his folks. They said his beautiful cousin had just died.

He put the phone down and stood there a minute looking out the window at Las Vegas.

"Charlie," he said, "I don't think I can stand to see another member of my family die like this.

"I think I'd rather go first myself."

Elvis was always fascinated with the kind of life that follows death. In a lot of pictures of him getting on his plane during a tour, you see him carrying a book. It usually was a book that might cast some light on the afterlife.

It was a mystery and a challenge to him.

He looked for answers in the Bible. Mostly in the words of Jesus that his Bible carried in red letters. Many times, in early morning darkness, you could look in Elvis' bedroom and he would be sitting up in bed, propped by pillows, glasses sitting on his nose. The Bible in his lap. Slowly moving a big magnifying glass with a handle back and forth across the text.

I gave him the magnifying glass for Christmas one year. He always kept it by his bedside.

He would look up and see you standing there.

"Listen to this," he'd say. And he'd read something to you with a voice that seemed to come from some kind of stage or pulpit.

In Los Angeles I liked to browse in Pickwick Bookstores. They carried books on mysticism.

Elvis didn't believe in psychics, in automatic writings or

third eyes. Nothing like that. They annoyed him.

"Charlie," he'd say, "why do you waste your time on those people?"

"Elvis, I don't live my life that way but I like to see what they say about the future," I said. "That fascinates me."

Let Elvis get started talking about religion and nobody else would get a word in edgewise. So many times, I would have thoughts of my own to express. No chance. I would get so frustrated, waiting for a chance to say a word, that I would just get up and walk out of the room.

One day, he saw me walking out and he stopped and said, "Where are you going, Charlie?"

"Out to the barn," I said.

"The barn? How come?"

"To see if I can tell Rising Sun something," I said. "I got no chance of telling you."

He nearly fell over the back of the chair, laughing.

If we were driving down the highway and he got to talking religion, his foot would slowly let off the gas. Finally , he would just be going along about 20 miles an hour and just talking up a storm.

You'd have to keep telling him to drive faster. He'd drive faster awhile, then start slowing down again.

"Here's What Blows Your Mind..."

One of those little books he often took on board the Lisa Marie with him, to read between concert stops, was a little gold bound book of writings by Paramahansa Yogananda, one of the Indian yogis so popular in Southern California.

Elvis first read about the yogi when Larry Geller, Elvis' personal barber in the '60s, gave him a book, The Autobiography of a Yogi.

The yogi had accurately foretold the exact day of his own death.

"And here's what blows your mind," Elvis said. "The

morticians at Forest Lawn said—and it was in all the newspapers—they said the yogi lay out on display for 20 days and still didn't show any signs of decay. The skin was still perfect. Perfect."

Larry knew the yogi's secretary, an American woman who had taken the Indian name of Sri Daya Mata, or Reverend Mother. She was then heading up the Self-Realization Fellowship which the yogi had founded.

Larry wanted Elvis to meet her.

I told Elvis we could get in the car and drive up in the hills of Pasadena and see her at the ashram.

"Let's go," he said.

He didn't put anything off.

Daya Mata came down the stairs with a big warm smile. She saw Elvis and took him upstairs alone with her. The rest of us waited downstairs, me, Billy, Charlie and Jerry.

We looked at the portrait of the yogi hanging on one wall. We admired all the flowers and green plants. Studied the candles.

A restful place.

Elvis was carrying some rolled manuscripts under his arm when he came back downstairs with Daya Mata beside him. When he got in the limousine and pulled away from the ashram, I asked him what the manuscripts were all about.

Elvis tapped his knee with them. He said they were not for public eyes.

Charlie asked, "What did you talk about upstairs? You were gone long enough."

"I asked her why God had chosen me to be Elvis Presley," he said. He raised the manuscripts and looked at them. "She said I might find the answer in these."

Elvis spent a lot of time trying to find the answer to that question.

Elvis may have found a hint of the answer through a man named Bernard Benson.

Benson did not look like a mystic should. He did not wear long flowing robes. His hair did not come down over his chest.   Benson's clothes and manner were those of a wealthy English gentlemen, which he was. He looked slightly out of place in the crowded lobby of the Hilton Hotel the first night I saw him in Las Vegas. Dark velvet suit. Brilliant gray eyes. Gray flecked beard and a shock of hair that he seemed to ignore.

There was a kind of poetry about him but in his youth he had made a fortune in war weapons.

Now he was in Las Vegas as a man of peace.

His ancient chateau in the south of France was now a refuge for Bhuddists who had fled the Chinese communist armies pouring into Tibet.

Benson had come to Las Vegas to see if Elvis could be persuaded to help these same Bhuddists.

One night, after the last show at the Hilton, I came downstairs to get something to eat before turning in.

One of the fans saw me step off the elevator. He came running up to me as if he had known me all his life.

"Charlie, there's a guy from England that says he has to meet someone from Elvis' show," he said with breathy confidentiality. "Can you talk?"

"Yea. Sure. Where is he?"

He darted off. I followed him over to where Benson was sitting on a couch with his lovely young wife.

He jumped to his feet to shake hands and launch at once into the purpose of his coming to Las Vegas. He seemed to have a great sense of urgency about his mission.

While vacationing out in Hawaii, he had written a hauntingly strange book about a young singer who lived in ages past. The boy wandered across the world, longing to bring happiness to all mankind.

Then, in a later century, came another young minstrel who did sing to the whole world—with the magic of electronic communications and satellites. As death came over him, he realized that he was the same young singer who, in an earlier age, had wanted to sing to the whole world. Now, he knew that he had finally realized his ancient dream. His heart was filled with joy.

Benson called his book, The Minstrel.

"Elvis inspired it," Benson said. "One of our Tibetan lamas, staying at the chateau, saw Elvis performing from Hawaii, via satellite. He pointed to the screen and said, 'He is a good man.'"

He paused and leaned forward. "Does all this strike you as being a bit mystical?"

I shook my head. "Mr. Benson, my first guru was Yogi Rama Charaka."

This yogi had been a Chicago lawyer named William Walter Atkinson before turning to Eastern religion.

"This is fantastic," Benson said. "You see, I want Elvis to help the Bhuddist priests at my chateau. To find a person with Elvis' company who has an Eastern background is miraculous, beyond credibility."

"You can believe," I said, thinking that it was a real coincidence.

He wiped real tears from his eyes.

Then he pulled a white scarf from an inside pocket of his velvet jacket. With no preliminary explanation, he said, "When you visit a Tibetan priest, you must bring him a silk scarf. It is expected. The scarf looks like the ones Elvis gives to his people in the audience.

"You must fold the scarf in a special way, much the same way you fold them before giving them to Elvis.

"As you hand the scarf to the priest you allow it to unfold to its full length. The priest then puts the scarf to his lips and blesses it.

"Then he hands it to you. Or he may keep it."

Benson said Tibetan holy men bring joy and wisdom to men through the scarf ceremony.

"Elvis brings joy to all around him with his scarf ceremony on stage," he said.

I took his book, The Minstrel, and promised that Elvis would look at it.

Elvis saw it lying on his bedside table at Graceland, one day not long after. He opened it and studied the story and the little stick drawings made by Benson himself to illustrate it.

"Charlie, is this something for Lisa Marie?" he said.

I tried to explain to him what it was.

From time to time, I saw the book lying in different places around Elvis' upstairs suite at Graceland. The bedroom. The office. The toilet.

Elvis had responded to something he found in its pages and the spirit of the lively little stick drawings.

If he saw something prophetic in its ending, he chose to say nothing about it.

This Always Baffled Elvis...

There was something—or a lack of something—about the people around Elvis that always puzzled him.

He liked to use nicknames.

Hog Ears is what he liked to call Alan Fortas, foreman at the Circle G ranch. Pinhead is what he called Lamar. Slewfoot is what he called me, sometimes Waterhead. He had a nickname for everyone he liked. If he didn't know your name, he might just call you Chief.

We called him Crazy—because he had such a wild sense of humor. He loved it.

One afternoon in Las Vegas, Dr. Elias Ghanem came by Elvis' suite at the Hilton.

The shades had been pulled. Elvis was sitting in shadows. Dr. Ghanem was standing by him. They were talking.

Elvis looked up when I walked in.

"What do you want, Slewfoot?" he said.

"Not a thing," I said. "I just came in to see if you needed anything."

Elvis looked up at the dark-skinned doctor.

"Tell me, Doc," he said. "I can call Charlie anything I want to. He never gets mad. I don't hurt his feelings.

"The other guys would pout for days. Or years.

"Why the difference, Doc?"

Dr. Ghanem studied Elvis and shook his head.

It reminded me of something that happened in Hawaii on our last trip out there.

We had been on tour and had three weeks vacation coming up before we had to leave on the next tour. I wanted to spend the break in Hawaii—alone.

That night I got dressed for the concert and went down to Elvis' motel suite to fix his hair before we went to the auditorium. I always had to fix his hair before every show.

I got his hair washed and dried off with a motel towel and reached for the hair dryer.

"You know, Charlie," Elvis said, joking, "if I go bald, you're fired."

He leaned back with his eyes closed.

"I think I may take a couple of weeks and fly out to the Islands," I said. "At the end of the tour. Maybe by myself."

"Why go out by yourself?" Elvis asked.

"Oh, just to get away," I said. "Also, I plan to see Bernard Benson and his wife."

Sometimes, back in Memphis, I'd go down to the river alone when things got too tight. I'd just sit and look at the river awhile. When I got up and came back to Graceland I felt better.

Elvis got up and shook his head. "No, we're all going to be busy, making some records."

Well, that was that, I figured. No Hawaiian break.

No sooner had I left his suite than Elvis called in Joe.

"Joe," he said, "we're all going out to Hawaii. At the end of the tour. We all need a vacation. Set it up out there for all of us. Everybody can go along."

When Joe stopped by to tell me, I said, "I wanted to go out there all by myself."

Joe nodded. "He said you could go off on your own, see anybody you wanted to, once we get out there."

Joe flew on out to Hawaii ahead of us to rent the hotel and the house on the beach. To have cars and limousines waiting to take us there from the airport. Try to get hold of Sam and his big Cadillac.

My job was to stay behind and get 28 people around Graceland on the plane to Hawaii.

A few days later, we were all on the Lisa Marie, heading across the big Pacific.

Everybody seemed quieter than usual. Elvis spent most of the time back in his bedroom, going over books on religion. Dr. Nichopolous would drift back there and chat. So would Billy. I'd wander through. My room was next to his so that I was close when he needed me.

Coming in to land, I looked out a window and saw Joe standing down there with a whole line of limousines waiting.

We settled in at the beach house.

One afternoon, we were all down at the edge of the ocean, sitting on big towels. Lamar was walking down from the house, trying to step easy on the broken coral so it wouldn't hurt his bare feet so bad. Elvis watched him walk right on past us down the beach.

Elvis turned to Ginger Alden, sitting by him.

"Lamar just reminded me of something," he told her. He grinned at me. "I'll bet you remember this one, Charlie."

He glanced back down the beach at Lamar who was getting smaller in the distance.

"Lamar and Gee Gee decided they'd swim way out there around the reef and watch the fish," he said. "Then one of them got the idea they should swim out a little farther. Beyond the reef."

I began to hum the song, Beyond the Reef.

"Shut up, Charlie," Elvis said. "Anyway, they didn't know the ocean has a tidal current that can suck strong swimmers out to sea. It started taking them out. Fast. They liked to never got back inside the reef. It was a real struggle.

"Around sunset, I looked out there and saw some big something thrashing around. It was Lamar. By the time we went out in the edge of the water a ways to help them in, they were pooped.

"I said, 'Lamar, you looked like a great white whale out there.'

"Lamar said, 'Y'all never even looked up! We could have drowned out there! You never even looked up!'

"He was really mad at me."

"I Want To Go Back..."

Elvis grew more and more anxious to make a tour of England and Europe—especially Germany and France.

There was tension in his voice when he talked about it.

"I want to get back to Paris again, to Frankfort and Munich," he said. "I might even want to check out that vacant lot near the house in Bad Nauheim where we played touch football, with the guys who came over on weekends from my outfit. We could set up a game for everybody in our show."

"Can I play on Kathy Westmoreland's team?" I said.

He frowned. "If I had my gun handy, I'd shoot you."

I laughed. "Hey Elvis. Remember the time over there when we all got knives and cut our wrists and held them together and swore we were blood brothers for life?" I said.

He chuckled. "Yea, and how we all cheered when Lamar finally drew blood."

He was feeling better.

One night in Las Vegas, after the last show, I wandered into his suite. He was talking to Joe about the tour.

"We have to get a tour set up for Europe and England," he said. "I mean soon."

Joe nodded. "Well, the Colonel says Concerts West is

telling him that an Elvis show would have big problems overseas. Border guards going through all the luggage. Problems like that."

Concerts West was Elvis' booking agency.

"There's something else," Joe said. "They don't have too many halls and auditoriums over there that are big enough to make expenses on a show as big as yours. You would have to charge a lot of money for the ticket and you always refuse to do that."

Elvis shook his head.

"I don't want a high priced ticket to see me," He said. "I want the tickets cheap enough so all the fans can see me if they want to."

Joe nodded. "Over there, the food and hotel expenses and everything you have to have for 85 people on the road can run you about $60,000 a day, easy."

Elvis stood up.

"Money is not what this tour is all about, Joe," he said.

He picked up a long, thin cigar and rolled it thoughtfully between his thumb and fingers.

"If the Colonel doesn't hurry up and set a tour over there, I'm going to set one up myself," he said. He looked at Joe. "You tell the Colonel I said that."

Joe nodded. "I will, Elvis. I'll tell him."

Joe was caught between two dynamos—Elvis and the Colonel. All of us were.

Elvis' eyes had a haunted look in them.

"I have to go over there while I still look like what the fans think I look like," he said.

"I know," I said. "Joe will talk to the Colonel about it."

"I'm Almost Exhausted..."

The Stamps Quartet was singing one of those beautiful old gospel songs.

Elvis waited, not sipping mineral water as usual. He

leaned on Glenn's piano. His eyes seemed drained of power.

We were only half way through the first Showroom performance of the night.

"Charlie," he said, "I'm almost exhausted."

He was tired. That's all. That's what we all thought.

It was impossible to think of Elvis dying. After his death, they found that he had already suffered three heart attacks. His heart was severly damaged. Even then one side was now twice as big as it should have been. His liver problem was severe and deteriorating, the same as his mother's had been not long before she died. Elvis was taking medication for glaucoma. We all knew how hard Dr. Nichopolous was fighting Elvis' high blood pressure.

The quartet ended the hymn. Elvis straightened and strolled like a young tiger into the center of the spotlight. He wore a big smile.

"Charlie," he called out, "bring a stool out here. And bring me my guitar. I want to show these people I can still play it."

I brought the stool and Elvis sat down. He hooked the guitar strap over his shoulder and began to strum the strings. He tuned one string.

"See there?" he said to the audience.

They smiled and chuckled along with him.

He told them about the way it was in Memphis in the beginning. Not a lot of people up on stage with him then as there was now in the huge Showroom performance. In the early days, it was just Elvis up there with his acoustic guitar, Scotty Moore on electric guitar, Bill Black on bass. No drums then. J.D. Fontana and his drums came later.

The audience loved getting rock 'n roll history from the mouth of the King. They loved it and Elvis managed to grab a little rest so he could go ahead and finish the show.

He was just tired. That's what we thought.

But there was a free floating feeling of unease.

It showed up in the band when some of the guys began complaining that Elvis wasn't changing up the show enough to keep it alive and jumping. They said Elvis was standing in musical cement. They wanted to change. They told Elvis that his fans were tired of hearing the same old songs, over and over.

One night, I was washing and styling Elvis' hair before the show.

He closed his eyes as I rubbed his head with the towel. He asked me what I thought about all the complaints.

"Jimmy Wakely once warned me about switching a successful show around just because some of your backup men are getting used to it," I said. "The show they are tired of may be a brand new show to the people in your audience that night."

Elvis went to talk to the Colonel about it.

The Colonel listened. He spun his cigar and nodded.

"Elvis," he said, "maybe there is some way we can find out what the people want to hear when they come to the show."

"Tell you what, Colonel," Elvis said, "You have them put a suggestion box in the lobby, where folks pass on the way to the Showroom. Let them write down the name of any song they want to hear me sing that night. During the show, we'll stop and pull one of them out of the box and do it."

It was strange.

Every suggestion that came out of that box was for one of the regular songs that Elvis was already doing in the show.

Elvis only had trouble with two of the many hundreds of songs in our arrangement book. He recalled the words to all the others, letter perfect.

The two that gave him trouble were the second verse of "Just Can't Help Believing" and the first verse of "My Way."

He loved to play with the words in a song. Fans got a kick out of watching him do it. But some people wanted to say it proved that Elvis couldn't remember the words to his big songs anymore.

Some people see everything wrong. With some special twist.

They seem to have some strange axe to grind.

As The Years Went By...

Lots of the guys moved off the Hill as the years went by.

Billy and Mike and some of the others moved away so they could have more time to spend with their children while they were growing up.

There was no longer the same hustle and bustle of the early days.

One night, Elvis came downstairs, dressed to the hilt. He came back in the kitchen.

"Mr. Elvis, you going out tonight?" Mary Jenkins asked him.

Elvis leaned in the doorway. "Naw, Mary. I thought I would just dress up for you guys back here."

"Well, just sit right down at that table and I'll bring you something real nice," Mary said.

We made a little party out of it.

After a while, Elvis didn't want me to get out of his sight for very long at a time.

One Christmas he looked in my room and saw me packing. I was going down to Decatur for the holidays. Elvis looked a little put out with me.

"Charlie," he said, "I hope you don't get to where you go off like this every Christmas that rolls around. You did the same thing last year."

"Elvis," I said, tossing rolled sox into my suitcase. "I'm going to spend a couple of days with my parents. It's my mother and father and you know how old my father is getting."

He thought about it. "Yea. Well, that's a good thing to do."

He walked down the hall.

Christmas at Graceland

Elvis wanted all his friends and relatives around him at Christmas. Bill Morris, later the sheriff and county mayor, was at one of the early Christmasses at Graceland that Elvis loved so much:

Elvis bought his first bunch of Graceland Christmas cards from me. I was with a printing company. It was a green and white snow scene. It said, "Merry Christmas From Graceland."

Elvis always wanted all of his uncles and aunts and cousins and grandparents up on the Hill around him at Christmas.

"I love every one of them," he said. "I can never replace them."'

He gave away millions in cars, jewels, horses, boats, dogs. He supported 50 charities in Memphis alone. Even when he was a poor kid in Tupelo he'd give away what little toys he got to make other kids happy.

One year when I was up on the Hill for Christmas, Elvis had put decorated Christmas trees in every room on the Hill. Every shelf in sight was loaded with pies and cakes and homemade candies. A pack of screaming children ran through the house, chasing after a dozen little puppies that Elvis had gone out and bought for them all. Lisa Marie led the pack. Folks packed the house and spilled out the doors.

Elvis' fans were down at the gate having a party of their own.

I discovered Elvis outside. Behind the mansion.

He was shining a powerful flashlight up among the bare limbs of the trees at colorful peacocks roosting up there. Little beady eyes reflected his flashlight beam.

Elvis swung the light down across his bunch of motorcycles, funny buggies and cars—and a big new Mercedes parked behind the house.

"Like the Mercedes?" he said.

"It's a beauty." I said.
"It's yours," he said.
He grinned at my total surprise.
"Merry Christmas, Bill," he said.

Elvis loved his peacocks at Graceland. But there was a couple of the birds that scared you in the dark of the night with that scream that sounded so human.

If it ever got too quiet on the Hill, Elvis would call out to the barn and ask Mike, "Where did the peacocks go?"

There was only one peacock that Elvis didn't like. It liked to fly down out of the trees and sit on his Rolls Royce and look at its reflection in the shiny surface—and scratch at it with its claws.

Elvis always got a kick out of picking out a surprise Christman gift for the guys. One year he got us all electric clocks that projected the time up on the dark ceiling. You could lie there and just open your eyes and look up on the ceiling and see what time it was. You could reach out and touch a button and a sexy female voice would say something like, "It's one o'clock and time to get up."

It was hard to find something to give Elvis. One year we all chipped in and gave him a life sized statue of Jesus. Elvis put it down in the Meditation Garden and it's still there. It had a plaque on it with all our names.

One night, Elvis got mad at all of us and walked off down to the Meditation Garden.

When he came back, he said the plaque was broken.

"God must have broken it to show me I shouldn't get angry at you," he said.

One of the funniest things that ever happened at Christmas was something Richard Davis told me about:

One Christmas, Elvis sent me out to buy $5,000 worth of fireworks, over in Arkansas. We chose up sides at night and had fireworks shootouts in the field behind the mansion. The sky would blaze with the celestial firepower.

One of the kinds of fireworks I bought was Cracker Balls,

little round things the size of your fingernail. They came in all colors and they looked a lot like M & M candy.

We put a bowl of them in the kitchen, near a little eating table.

I was talking with one of the guys and the cook was going to town on something.

Vernon Presley was notorious for walking into the kitchen and taking off the lid of whatever was cooking and slurping several big tastes.

Vernon came in and saw the colorful bowl of Cracker Balls and scooped up a couple and threw them in his mouth and chomped down on them.

We heard a muffled "thomp."

We turned around, Vernon's eyes were bulging out of their sockets. Smoke was coming out his mouth with bits of paper stuck between his teeth.

He stayed there in the kitchen all day long. He kept trying to get somebody else to eat some.

Everybody who came in, he'd pick up the bowl and say, "Want some M & Ms?"

Loneliness Drifts In

But as more and more people left the hill, the air of loneliness drifted into other rooms.

One night we were recording a new album at Graceland. Felton Jarvis came down from Nashville long enough to produce it. He and I were sitting on the steps of the den, listening to Elvis working on a song. Working hard and alone.

Some of the guys were out in the dining room. Playing cards.

The control room was set up in a trailer out back, where all of Elvis' cars were parked.

All the daytime people who worked around Graceland were gone.

"You know, Felton," I said, "I can remember the time when every one of the guys would have been in here. Pulling for Elvis. Cheering him on. Ready to break loose and celebrate every good cut Elvis came through with.

"Now, it's just Elvis in there working with the voices and me and you sitting out here."

Felton looked around. "It's not like it used to be."

Elvis got tired. "Let's call it a night, fellows," he said.

He headed upstairs by himself.

I went by his bedroom later to say good night. He seemed low.

"You okay, Elvis?" I said.

He twirled the glass of water on his bedside table.

"They've started treating me like a chunk of meat," he said. "They keep me cool. When it's time to go out on the road they all come in from Nashville and here and there and pick me up and deliver me on the stage. When the tour is over, they deliver me back home to Graceland and go their separate ways again.

"Until next time."

I sat down on the end of his bed. He didn't look at me.

"Things will be better, Elvis," I said. "Things go through phases."

He was silent a long time. I just waited.

Then he began slowly flexing his fingers and rubbing them.

"What is wrong?" I said.

He moved his shoulders and winced slightly. "I don't know. There's pain all over my body. I can feel it a lot in my hands and up in my shoulder tonight."

Elvis had asked several people in recent months to rub his back and arms with a white lotion he kept in his bathroom.

"I don't know what it is," Elvis said.

The mystery of the pain was cleared up for me one day, a few months after Elvis died.

I was still living at Graceland and I went by to visit Elvis father, Vernon, who had become quite ill. There was a knock at the door and when I opened it Dr. Nichopoulous walked in.

Dr. Nichopolous asked Vernon about his health and what was being done for him.

Then he shocked both of us. He said what he was about to tell us must be kept in strictest confidence. He said that during the autopsy it was discovered that Elvis had bone cancer that had spread through his entire body.

"You Have To Come Now..."

One night after that recording session, I called Larry Geller in Hollywood.

"Elvis wants to know when you're coming in," I said.

"Well, I'm working on a deal to promote my own hair care products now," Larry said.

Elvis was listening on his upstairs phone. He often did that.

"You have to come on in now, Larry," he said.

He gave Larry a long list of books to bring him. One of them was the story of the Shroud of Turin. It told of a shroud that bore the image of a person thought to be Christ. The image was mysteriously imprinted, possibly by a nuclear event of some kind. Many thought the shroud had been the one which was used to wrap the body of Jesus after he was taken down from the cross. The image was thought to be the result of some cosmic force that brought Jesus back to life.

Larry didn't come right away. I called him back on August 15, 1977.

Larry tied up the ends of a business deal and hurried to Memphis. I met him downstairs at Graceland and took the books from him that he had brought in from Hollywood.

"Elvis is sleeping upstairs, Larry," I said. "I'll put them by his bedside. He'll see them when he wakes up."

Larry pulled out the one about the Shroud of Turin and put it on top of the stack.

"I have a feeling Elvis expects to find something he's been looking for in this one," he said. "I hope he finds it."

187

"He will," I said.
I had the distinct feeling he would.
This was the last book Elvis read.

"I Had a Dream..."'

A couple of days before we were to all fly up to Portland, Maine to open another sold-out tour, me and Elvis were going over some new music he wanted to put in the show.

He stopped singing and sipped some mineral water I had on the piano top for him.

"Charlie, do you remember that old song, 'One Sided Love Affair?'" he asked.

"Sure do." I hummed a couple of bars. "We could harmonize on that one. Want to do it in Portland?"

He shook his head, no. "I think that's what I've got on my hands," he said. "With Ginger. I had a dream about that song last night."

"What kind of dream?" I said.

"I dreamed I was singing the song on this tour that's coming up," he said. "That means I'm never going to marry her."

He put down the music and flipped through the pages of his book about the Shroud of Turin.

You could tell his time with Ginger was over.

I stood in the doorway of his bedroom several minutes, watching him reading his new book with such fascination. Slowly turning the pages.

Perhaps he was finding something he had been searching for after all.

"He Came Back To Some Of Us..."

Elvis went away.

But he came back to some of us one night in California.

189

Lindalee remembers that night:

A lot of guys in Elvis' stage band will tell you Elvis came back that night.

If it only happened in our mind, it's still okay.

Daddy had one more recording session with the boys, just before he died. They were the same guys he did his recording sessions with earlier, when they were not out on the road with Elvis.

There was Charlie Hodge, Glenn D. Hardin, Ronnie Tutt, Jerry Sheff and James Burton. Charlie was going to coach the voices.

It was all going to come down in one of Larry Muhoberac's recording studios out in the valley. Larry played for Elvis in the first show at the International Hotel.

The guys started coming in. They saw each other and got real big smiles on their faces with just a shadow of sadness.

They couldn't stop smiling. They hugged and hugged each other. Elvis was famous for always coming in a studio and hugging people. So they were carrying on some of his same spirit.

And they knew it.

When Charlie Hodge strolled in, it tore everybody up again.

Daddy finally got them organized and working. I was smiling so hard it hurt.

Charlie came in the control booth and hugged on me.

"I haven't been this happy in a long time, Lindalee," he said.

We stood there hugging each other. Holding on hard.

"Charlie, why do I feel so happy but my heart is breaking?" I said. "Is it because Elvis is not here in the studio with us?"

Charlie just smiled. "No, Lindalee. It's because Elvis IS here with us. Right now. Can't you feel his love?"

Daddy was a good Christian. He didn't believe in strange things like mystical third eyes and the dead coming back. But when he came in the booth I said, "Daddy, I'm on some kind of spiritual high. Do you feel it?"

He put his music on a stand and his arms went around me.

"I feel it, too, Lindalee," he said. "I feel it, too. The only thing we're missing is Elvis himself."

"He's not missing, Daddy," I said. "He came in with Charlie."

Jimmy died not long after that recording session.

Lindalee said, "I think that when Daddy crossed over and went through the light, Elvis was there, saying "Welcome home, Mr. Wakely. Let's go get our guitars."

"And Daddy looks like he did long ago. Elvis is that big piece of good looking meat.

"And they're doing harmony that is fantastic."

Time to say goodbye...

Some say it's time to say goodby to Elvis. It's time to move on, to get on with your life—the time has come to forget.

Of course, no time is right for forgetting the great people of our history—especially when we have lived part of our lives in their own era.

People remember—and always will.

Millions are coming to visit Graceland. Some of them only came to know Elvis through his movies—they were too young to see him while he was here.

His name has become a popular one for babies. I was a house guest of an English couple, Barry White and his wife, in Norwich. Their lovely child is named Elvisa.

Robert and Linda Barnett flew me up to their home in Schofield, Wisconsin to act as godfather at the christening of their son by Rev. Donald Berg in the lovely St. Theresa Catholic Church. The good Father pointed out that, as I am a Baptist, love can cross religious lines with ease. The Barnetts christened their son Aaron Elvis Barnett.

A medical center stands in Memphis in honor of Elvis. His statues stand on at least two continents. It was my pleasure to unveil them.

Many of the States now have an Elvis Memorial Day. More states are added each year.

There are scholarly studies and annual seminars on the magic and mystery of Elvis. There are memorial karate tournaments and joggers marathons to raise money for charity.

The list of good reasons to remember such a man as Elvis goes on. There is no end.

It is right that this is so.

Such human beings should not be forgotten. The best of their lives should live on as an inspiration—in a world that needs inspiration.

Yet, if one remembers—there is a time of loneliness.

Spending so many hours remembering Elvis, for the purpose of writing this book, has created loneliness in me like a torment.

But I would not have missed my time with Elvis for the rest of life itself. For it outweighed all the rest.

Now the work is over and I have only to say, as Elvis did, "Until we meet again, God bless you."

For additional copies of this special edition, send $7.95 for paperback or $13.95 for hardback plus a dollar for postage and handling to: Castle Books, P.O. Box 12506, Memphis, Tenn., 38182, USA. Cash, money order or cashiers' check accepted.

Regular editions of Castle Books publications are available at special discount rates for quantity purchases. Direct your enquiries to Special Marketing Department, Castle Books, Inc., Mail: P.O. Box 12506, Memphis, Tenn., 38182.

By Charlie Hodge with Charles Goodman